QUICK AND EASY AFTER WORK COOKBOOK

by Chrissie Taylor

foulsham

London . New York . Toronto . Sydney

ACKNOWLEDGEMENTS

With special thanks to Vera, my aunt, who thought her
typing days were over when she retired. How wrong
she was and I am very grateful for her skill in deciphering
my hand writing to type my manuscript.

I dedicate this book to Bruce with love. Your backing and
understanding gave me the encouragement to pursue what
would have remained a dream. Thank you for helping me
to make this book possible.

For my daughter, Sophie – love Mum.

foulsham

Bennetts Close, Cippenham, Berkshire SL1 5AP

ISBN 0-572-01804-5

Printed in Great Britain by
Cox & Wyman Ltd, Reading

CONTENTS

Introduction

Because of our change in lifestyle and eating habits, far more convenience foods are being used and are being introduced on the supermarket shelves than ever before. Consumers are able to buy complete meals just to reheat in the microwave or oven. These are great time-savers and we should not disregard them. But what about the consumer who wants a wholesome meal but hasn't the time to prepare it from fresh produce? Also to be considered are the consumers who want to present a first class meal but do not have the know-how or simply loathe cooking.

Many other factors have contributed to the changes. Often both husband and wife of families now work and single parents have full-time employment, thus leaving themselves with less leisure time.

This is where convenience foods come into their own category and should not be dismissed with any shame.

Garnishes and decoration of starters, main meals or sweets also play a vital part in the presentation of a meal and are almost as important as the ingredients used in the recipe. TO LOOK GOOD - TASTES GOOD and you are halfway there.

If I can try to define what a convenience food is, as most people would just consider them to be canned, frozen or out of a packet: A convenience food is anything that has been partially or completely prepared to make life easier for you in preparing a meal.

As an experienced chef, I understand the problems of a novice without the knowledge of catering skills. For this reason, use convenience foods to your advantage and together with the right combination of ingredients, coupled with the finished presentation, the compliments will come rolling in.

The ingredients for the recipes in this book I think most people would have in a store cupboard/freezer. Therefore the cook need not have to go on a special shopping trip or have any great culinary skills in presenting a first class meal.

Some casseroles and longer cooking dishes have been included as onces the quick preparation is completed you can put the dish in the oven and forget it for a while.

New recipes are now endless because of the range of so many convenience foods, so don't be afraid to experiment.

This book includes some recipes that I would like to share with you.

BON APPETIT!

NOTES FOR COOKS

• It is important that either metric, imperial or American measures are followed in all recipes, not a combination.

Spoon measures:

1 level tablespoon - 15ml

1 level teaspoon - 5ml

Spoon measurements in all recipes are level.

• When herbs are used in a recipe, the flavour of dried is stronger than fresh, so use half the quantity of dried. (Unless stated otherwise, dried herbs are used in all the recipes in this book.)

• Parsley, however, is probably the one herb that cannot be substituted by the dried ingredient. The difference in taste of dried parsley when used in a cooked recipe is hardly noticeable, but it does not have the same flavour or appearance when used as a garnish for dishes. Either chop or leave in sprigs to add the finishing touch to starters and soups, main courses, vegetables or salads. A bunch of parsley placed in a glass of water and left in a cool place will keep fresh for about 1 week.

• Garlic purée is also a good substitute for the fresh ingredient and a tube will keep for several weeks in the refrigerator once opened.

• The range in size of canned and packet produce varies enormously; so you need not be too precise when shopping for ingredients. Do not worry if a can size varies by a few grammes or ounces as it will not have any great bearing on the quality of the finished dish. However, discretion must be used. If a recipe states use a 30g/½ pint/1¼ cup packet mix of sauce, it could have disastrous effects if a 60g/1 pint/2½ cup mix is used. The liquid content would be too great in proportion to the other ingredients.

• When using the oven, cook on the centre shelf unless otherwise stated.

• **All recipes are for 4 servings.**

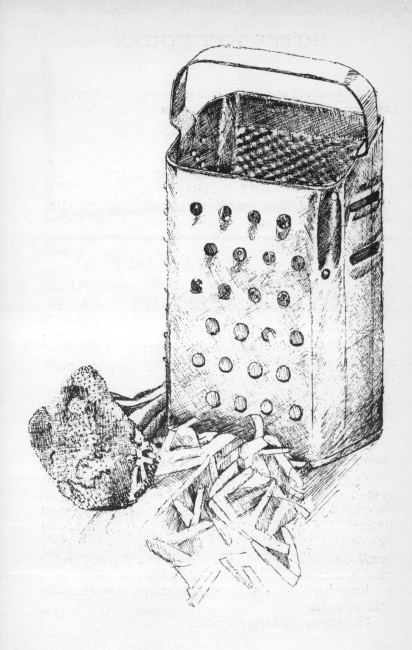

Soups

BEANY PASTA SOUP

ingredients	Metric	Imperial	American
Butter	25 g	1 oz	2 tbsp
Medium onion, chopped	1	1	1
Green or red bell pepper, chopped	½	½	½
Milk	750 ml	1¼ pts	3 cups
Can beans, such as kidney, haricot (navy) or a mixture, drained	450 g	1 lb	1 lb
Pasta, cooked	100 g	4 oz	1 cup
Salt and pepper			

method

1. Melt the butter in a pan and sauté the onion and pepper until golden brown. Add the milk and bring to the boil.

2. Add the beans, pasta and seasoning. Simmer for 2 minutes. Serve with crusty brown bread or granary French stick.

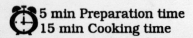 5 min Preparation time
15 min Cooking time

8

CARROT AND ORANGE SOUP

ingredients	Metric	Imperial	American
Carrots	450 g	1 lb	1 lb
Medium onion	1	1	1
Milk	300 ml	½ pt	1¼ cups
Chicken stock	300 ml	½ pt	1¼ cups
Salt and pepper			
Grated rind and juice of 1 orange			
Single (light) cream	150 ml	¼ pt	⅔ cup
Garnish:			
Chopped fresh parsley			

method

1. Chop the carrots and onion (a food processor will save time). Place in a saucepan with the milk, stock and seasoning. Simmer until tender.

2. Sieve or blend. Return to the saucepan, stir in the orange rind and juice and reheat gently but do not boil. Stir in the cream before serving. Garnish with chopped parsley. This soup may be served hot or cold.

note

If the soup is to be reheated, do not add the orange rind and juice until serving as it could curdle.

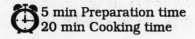 5 min Preparation time
20 min Cooking time

CHICKEN AND CORN SOUP

ingredients	Metric	Imperial	American
Chicken stock	600 ml	1 pt	2½ cups
Cooked chicken, diced	100 g	4 oz	⅔ cup
Can sweetcorn (corn kernels), drained	350 g	12 oz	12 oz
Dry sherry	2 tbsp	2 tbsp	2 tbsp

method

1. Place all the ingredients, except the sherry, in a pan and heat until boiling. Reduce heat to a simmer.

2. Stir in the sherry and serve with bread rolls.

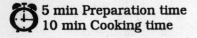 5 min Preparation time
10 min Cooking time

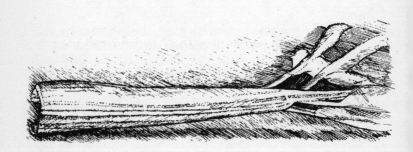

CHILLED CUCUMBER AND MINT SOUP

ingredients	Metric	Imperial	American
Medium cucumber, grated or finely chopped	1	1	1
Natural yoghurt	300 ml	½ pt	1¼ cups
Chopped fresh mint	1 tbsp	1 tbsp	1 tbsp
Wine vinegar	2 tbsp	2 tbsp	2 tbsp
Salt and pepper			
Milk	300 ml	½ pt	1¼ cups
Cream	2 tbsp	2 tbsp	2 tbsp
Garnish:			
Mint sprigs	4	4	4

method

1. Place the cucumber in a bowl, stir in the yoghurt, mint, wine vinegar and seasoning. Chill for at least 1 hour.

2. Stir in the milk just before serving. Pour into bowls and dribble a little cream in the centre. Swirl with a skewer or cocktail stick (toothpick) and garnish with a sprig of mint.

variation

Substitute the mint with chopped fresh parsley or chives.

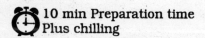 10 min Preparation time
Plus chilling

COLD CELERY AND MINT SOUP

ingredients	Metric	Imperial	American
Can condensed celery soup	425 g	15 oz	15 oz
Single (light) cream	150 ml	¼ pt	⅔ cup
Cucumber, roughly chopped	½	½	½
Mint sprigs	5	5	5
Salt and pepper			

method

1. Empty the soup into a blender or food processor.

2. Add the cream and cucumber. Reserve 8 mint leaves for garnish, add the rest to the cream and cucumber, season and process until smooth.

3. Pour into dishes or glasses and chill thoroughly. Garnish with the reserved mint leaves before serving.

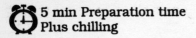 5 min Preparation time
Plus chilling

CRAB BISQUE

ingredients	Metric	Imperial	American
Butter	25 g	1 oz	2 tbsp
Medium onion, grated	1	1	1
Can cream of vegetable soup	2	2	2
Fish stock	30 ml	½ pt	1¼ cups
Light and dark crab meat (fresh, frozen or canned)	175g	6 oz	¾ cup
Salt and pepper			
Dry sherry	2 tbsp	2 tbsp	2 tbsp
Garnish:			
Chopped fresh parsley			
Croûtons			

method

1. Melt the butter in a pan and sauté the onion until soft.

2. Add the soup, stock and crab meat. Bring to simmering point, cover and cook for 10 minutes.

3. Season to taste and stir in the sherry. Serve in soup bowls with a sprinkling of parsley and croûtons.

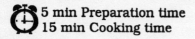 5 min Preparation time
15 min Cooking time

13

CREAMY CRAB SOUP

ingredients	Metric	Imperial	American
Cooked white or brown rice	100 g	4 oz	¾ cup
Milk	300 ml	½ pt	1 ¼ cups
Can crab meat	100 g	4 oz	4 oz
Fish stock	600 ml	1 pt	2 ½ cups
Salt and pepper			
Lemon juice	1 tbsp	1 tbsp	1 tbsp
Single (light) cream	150 ml	¼ pt	⅔ cup
Garnish:			
Paprika			
Chopped fresh parsley			

method

1. Place the rice, milk, crab, stock and seasoning in a pan and bring slowly to the boil, stirring.

2. Simmer gently for 5 minutes. Add the lemon juice and cream.

3. Place in soup bowls and sprinkle with a little paprika and parsley. Serve with prawn or rice crackers.

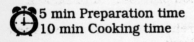

5 min Preparation time
10 min Cooking time

CREAM OF CAULIFLOWER SOUP

ingredients	Metric	Imperial	American
Butter	25 g	1 oz	2 tbsp
Small cauliflower, broken into florets	1	1	1
Small onion, chopped	1	1	1
Milk	750 ml	1¼ pts	3 cups
Celery salt or 1 fresh stick, chopped	½ tsp	½ tsp	½ tsp
Salt and pepper			
Garnish:			
Chopped fresh parsley			
Croûtons			

method

1. Melt the butter in a pan and sauté the cauliflower and onion until lightly browned.

2. Add the milk and seasonings and simmer for 10-15 minutes until the cauliflower is tender.

3. Blend or purée in a food processor until smooth.

4. Return to the pan, reheat and serve garnished with parsley and croûtons.

10-15 min Preparation time
10-15 min Cooking time

CURRIED CARROT SOUP

ingredients	Metric	Imperial	American
Butter	25 g	1 oz	2 tbsp
Carrots, sliced	450 g	1 lb	1 lb
Onions, chopped	225 g	8 oz	2 cups
Vegetable stock	900 ml	1½ pts	3¾ cups
Curry powder	1 tbsp	1 tbsp	1 tbsp
Salt and pepper			
Garnish:			
Chopped fresh parsley			
Croûtons			

method

1. Melt the butter in a pan and sauté the carrots and onions until lightly browned.

2. Add the stock and curry powder. Cook for 10-15 minutes until the vegetables are tender.

3. Blend or purée in a food processor and adjust the seasoning.

4. Reheat and serve sprinkled with parsley and croûtons.

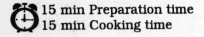
15 min Preparation time
15 min Cooking time

FRANKFURTER AND ONION SOUP

ingredients	Metric	Imperial	American
425g /15 oz cans French onion soup	3	3	3
Jar frankfurters	350 g	12 oz	12 oz
Garnish:			
Croûtons	50 g	2 oz	2 oz

method

1. Heat the soup in a pan until boiling.

2. Slice the frankfurters, add to the soup and simmer gently to heat through. Serve sprinkled with croûtons.

5 min Preparation time
5 min Cooking time

PARSLEY SOUP

ingredients	Metric	Imperial	American
Fresh parsley, chopped	100 g	4 oz	3 cups
Medium onion, chopped	1	1	1
Large potato, chopped	1	1	1
Vegetable stock	300 ml	½ pt	1¼ cups
Cornflour (cornstarch)	25 g	1 oz	¼ cup
Milk	300 ml	½ pt	1¼ cups
Salt and pepper			
Single (light) cream	150 ml	¼ pt	⅔ cup

method

1. Place the parsley, onion, potato and stock in a pan and simmer for 20 minutes. Cool slightly.

2. Blend or purée in a food processor until smooth.

3. Mix the cornflour with a little of the milk. Return the soup to the pan, add the milk and seasoning and bring to the boil.

4. Stir in the cornflour paste and simmer, stirring continuously, until thickend.

5. Swirl the cream through before serving. Serve with Melba toast or croûtons. This soup may also be served chilled.

5-10 min Preparation time
25-30 min Cooking time

PEA AND FRANKFURTER SOUP

ingredients	Metric	Imperial	American
425g /15 oz cans condensed pea and ham soup	2	2	2
Milk	300 ml	½ pt	1¼ cups
Jar frankfurters	350 g	12 oz	12 oz
Salt and pepper			

method

1. Place the soup and milk in a saucepan. Stir well to combine and heat until boiling.

2. Slice the frankfurters, add to the soup and simmer gently until heated through. Season to taste.

3. Serve with crusty French bread or rolls.

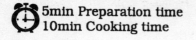 5min Preparation time
10min Cooking time

STARTERS

ALPINE GRAPEFRUIT

ingredients	Metric	Imperial	American
Can grapefruit segments, drained	450 g	1 lb	1 lb
Muesli (granola)	75 g	3 oz	1 cup
Natural yoghurt	150 ml	¼ pt	⅔ cup
Soft brown sugar			

method

1. Place the grapefruit segments in a bowl. Add the muesli and bind together with yoghurt.

2. Divide between 4 dishes and sprinkle with brown sugar.

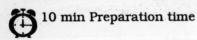 10 min Preparation time

AVOCADO DIP

ingredients	Metric	Imperial	American
Avocado	1	1	1
Cream cheese	100 g	4 oz	½ cup
Single (light) cream	4 tbsp	4 tbsp	4 tbsp
Clove garlic, crushed, or 1 tsp garlic purée	1	1	1
Squeeze of lemon juice			
Salt and pepper			

method

1. Cut the avocado in half. Remove the stone (pit) and scoop out the flesh with a spoon.

2. Place all the ingredients in a blender or a food processor and mix until smooth.

3. Pour into a dish and chill. Serve with crudités such as blanched cauliflower florets, carrot, celery and cucumber sticks, radishes or savoury crisps or with Melba toast.

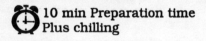 10 min Preparation time
Plus chilling

AVOCADO AND PRAWN COCKTAIL

ingredients	Metric	Imperial	American
Avocado, peeled and diced	1	1	1
Prawns (shrimp), fresh or frozen	100 g	4 oz	⅔ cup
Cucumber, diced	¼	¼	¼
Grated rind of 1 lemon			
Soured (dairy sour) cream	3 tbsp	3 tbsp	3 tbsp
Natural yoghurt	3 tbsp	3 tbsp	3 tbsp
Salt and pepper			
Garnish:			
Lettuce leaves			
Lemon slices			

method

1. Place the avocado, prawns, reserving a few for garnish, cucumber and lemon rind in a bowl.

2. Stir in the soured cream and yoghurt. Season to taste.

3. Shred the lettuce leaves and place in the bottom of 4 glasses or shallow dishes. Pile the avocado mixture on top.

4. Garnish with lemon slices and the reserved prawns. Serve chilled.

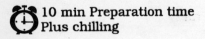 10 min Preparation time
Plus chilling

22

AVOCADO RAREBIT SHELLS

ingredients	Metric	Imperial	American
Ripe avocados	2	2	2
Lemon juice	2 tsp	2 tsp	2 tsp
Packet white sauce mix	300 ml	½ pt	1¼ cups
Horseradish sauce	1 tsp	1 tsp	1 tsp
Cheddar cheese, cut into small dice	100 g	4 oz	1 cup
Grated parmesan cheese	1 tbsp	1 tbsp	1 tbsp
Garnish:			
Chopped fresh parsley			

method

1. Halve and stone (pit) the avocados. Dice the flesh, reserving the shells. Place the avocado flesh in a bowl and toss in the lemon juice to prevent discoloration.

2. Make up the white sauce mix according to directions and add the horseradish sauce, Cheddar cheese and avocado flesh.

3. Pile into the reserved shells or ramekin dishes and sprinkle with Parmesan. Flash under a hot grill (broiler) to brown the surface. Serve immediately garnished with parsley.

variation

Use diced ham in place of cheese.

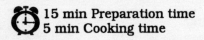
15 min Preparation time
5 min Cooking time

BRANDIED CHICKEN LIVER PATE

ingredients	Metric	Imperial	American
Butter	50 g	2 oz	¼ cup
Medium onion, chopped	1	1	1
Chicken livers, chopped	450 g	1 lb	1 lb
Garlic purée	1 tsp	1 tsp	1 tsp
Mixed herbs	1 tsp	1 tsp	1 tsp
Brandy	2 tbsp	2 tbsp	2 tbsp
Double (heavy) cream	150 ml	¼ pt	⅔ cup
Salt and pepper			
Garnish:			
Lemon wedges			
Parsley sprigs			

method

1. Melt the butter in a pan and sauté the onion and livers gently until the meat is sealed.

2. Add the garlic purée and herbs, cover and cook gently for 10-15 minutes until the livers are cooked, stirring occasionally.

3. Place in a blender or food processor, add the brandy and cream and mix until smooth. Adjust the seasoning to taste.

4. Pour into individual dishes or one large dish and chill until firm. Garnish with lemon wedges and parsley and serve with Melba toast.

5 min Preparation time
20 min Cooking time
Plus chilling

CHEESE AND HERB DIP

ingredients	Metric	Imperial	American
Cheddar or Cheshire cheese, grated	100 g	4 oz	1 cup
Cream cheese	100 g	4 oz	½ cup
Single (light) or pouring (coffee) cream	150 ml	¼ pt	⅔ cup
Clove garlic, crushed, or 1 tsp garlic purée	1	1	1
Chopped fresh parsley	1 tsp	1 tsp	1 tsp
Mint	1 tsp	1 tsp	1 tsp
Salt and pepper			

method

1. Place all the ingredients in a blender or food processor and mix until smooth.

2. Pour into a dish and chill. Serve in the centre of a large plate surrounded with crudités, such as cauliflower florets, carrot, celery and cucumber sticks, radishes or savoury crisps.

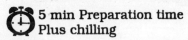 5 min Preparation time
Plus chilling

CHEESE STUFFED EGGS

ingredients	Metric	Imperial	American
Hard-boiled (hard-cooked) eggs	4	4	4
Cream cheese	50 g	2 oz	¼ cup
Mayonnaise	1 tbsp	1 tbsp	1 tbsp
Salt and pepper			
Garnish:			
Paprika			
Lettuce leaves			

method

1. Halve the eggs, remove the yolks and sieve.

2. Add the cheese, mayonnaise and seasoning to the yolks and mix until smooth.

3. Pipe or spoon into the egg white halves and sprinkle with paprika. Serve chilled on a bed of lettuce.

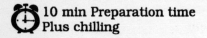 10 min Preparation time
Plus chilling

DEVILLED DIP

ingredients	Metric	Imperial	American
Cream cheese	225 g	8 oz	1 cup
Single (light) cream	150 ml	¼ pt	⅔ cup
Green bell pepper	½	½	½
Red bell pepper	½	½	½
Tabasco (hot pepper) sauce	¼ tsp	¼ tsp	¼ tsp
Worcestershire sauce	1 tbsp	1 tbsp	1 tbsp
Garnish:			
Chopped fresh parsley			

method

1. Place all the ingredients into a blender or food processor and mix well until thickened.

2. Pour into a bowl and chill.

3. Sprinkle with chopped parsley and serve with crudités such as carrot, celery and cucumber sticks, grissini sticks and biscuits (crackers).

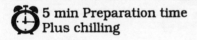 5 min Preparation time
Plus chilling

KIPPER PATE

ingredients	Metric	Imperial	American
Packet kipper fillets with butter	225 g	8 oz	8 oz
Lemon juice	1 tbsp	1 tbsp	1 tbsp
Mayonnaise	2 tbsp	2 tbsp	2 tbsp
Black pepper			
Garnish:			
Lemon wedges			
Parsley sprigs			

method

1. Cook the kippers according to the directions. Place in a bowl with the juices and remove the kipper skin.

2. Add the lemon juice and mash together until smooth. Add the mayonnaise and pepper and mix well.

3. Place in a serving dish or individual ramekins and chill. Garnish with lemon wedges and a sprig of parsley before serving. Serve with crispbreads or toast.

variation

Fresh cream may be used instead of mayonnaise. The pâté will be slightly softer and have less bite.

⏰ 5-10 min Preparation time
10 min Cooking time
Plus chilling

MELON BALLS WITH HAM AND GINGER SAUCE

ingredients	Metric	Imperial	American
Packet frozen melon balls, thawed	450 g	1 lb	1 lb
Shoulder ham, sliced and cut into thin strips	50 g	2 oz	2 oz
Natural yoghurt	150 ml	¼ pt	⅔ cup
Pieces stem ginger in syrup, chopped	4	4	4
Ginger syrup	1 tbsp	1 tbsp	1 tbsp

method

1. Mix the melon balls with the ham and place in dishes or glasses.

2. Mix the yoghurt, ginger and syrup together and pour over the melon. Chill before serving.

variation

For a special occasion, substitute shoulder ham with Parma ham.

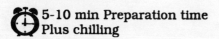 5-10 min Preparation time
Plus chilling

PATE DIP

ingredients	Metric	Imperial	American
Liver sausage	100 g	4 oz	½ cup
Cream cheese	100 g	4 oz	½ cup
Worcestershire sauce	1 tbsp	1 tbsp	1 tbsp
Single (light) or pouring (coffee) cream	5 tbsp	5 tbsp	5 tbsp
Mixed herbs	1 tsp	1 tsp	1 tsp
Salt and pepper			

method

1. Place all the ingredients in a blender or food processor and mix until smooth.

2. Pour into a dish and chill. Serve with crudités such as blanched cauliflower florets, carrot, celery and cucumber sticks, radishes or savoury crisps or Melba toast.

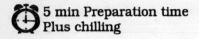 5 min Preparation time
Plus chilling

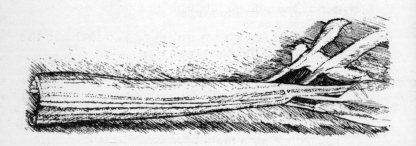

SALMON MOUSSE

ingredients	Metric	Imperial	American
Packet parsley sauce mix	300 ml	½ pt	1¼ cups
Lemon juice	1 tbsp	1 tbsp	1 tbsp
Can red or pink salmon, drained and flaked	425 g	15 oz	15 oz
Tomato purée (paste)	1 tbsp	1 tbsp	1 tbsp
Eggs, size 3, separated	2	2	2
Powdered gelatine	15 g	½ oz	½ oz
Salt and pepper			
Double (heavy) cream, whipped	150 ml	¼ pt	⅔ cup
Garnish:			
Fresh prawns (shrimp)			
Cucumber slices			
Stuffed olives, sliced			
Lemon slices			

method

1. Make up the sauce mix according to the directions.

2. Add the lemon juice, salmon, tomato purée and egg yolks. Mix well.

3. Dissolve the gelatine in 4 tablespoons water and add to the salmon mixture. Season to taste.

4. Whisk the egg whites until stiff and fold into the salmon with the cream.

5. Spoon into a salmon mould or 600 ml/1 pt/2 ½ cup soufflé dish and chill until set.

6. Turn out and garnish. This mousse may be served as a starter or a main course with salad.

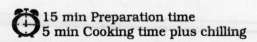
15 min Preparation time
5 min Cooking time plus chilling

31

Fish

CHEESE AND HADDOCK LAYER BAKE

ingredients	Metric	Imperial	American
Haddock, skinned	450 g	1 lb	1 lb
Can sliced mushrooms, drained	200 g	7 oz	7 oz
Salt and pepper			
Packet cheese sauce mix	300 ml	½ pt	1¼ cups
Small onion, finely chopped	1	1	1
Medium potatoes, thinly sliced	4	4	4
Butter, melted	25 g	1 oz	2 tbsp
Cheddar cheese, grated	25 g	1 oz	¼ cup
Garnish:			
Chopped fresh parsley			

method

1. Place the haddock in a dish and sprinkle over the mushrooms. Season.

2. Make up the sauce mix according to directions. Stir in the onion and pour over the fish.

3. Arrange the potato slices over the sauce, overlapping, but in a single layer.

4. Season, brush with melted butter and sprinkle with cheese. Bake in a preheated oven at 200°C/400°F/Gas Mark 6 for 50-60 minutes until golden brown and the potatoes are tender. Garnish with parsley before serving.

variation

Use cod instead of haddock.

 10-15 min Preparation time
50-60 min Cooking time

Cod Kebabs Flamenco

ingredients	Metric	Imperial	American
Cod, cut into 2.5cm / 1 inch cubes	225 g	8 oz	8 oz
Can pineapple cubes, drained	200 g	7 oz	7 oz
Button mushrooms	8	8	8
Tomatoes, cut into quarters	2	2	2
Butter, melted	25 g	1 oz	2 tbsp
Packet white sauce mix	300 ml	½ pt	1¼ cup
Tomato purée (paste)	1 tbsp	1 tbsp	1 tbsp
Few drops tabasco (hot pepper) sauce			

method

1. Thread 4 skewers alternately with fish, pineapple, mushrooms and tomatoes.

2. Place on a grill pan, brush with butter and grill (broil) on medium heat for about 10-15 minutes, turning regularly.

3. While the kebabs are cooking, make up the sauce mix according to the directions. Add the tomato purée and tabasco sauce.

4. Serve the kebabs with brown rice or jacket potatoes and the sauce.

variation

Use haddock or plaice instead of cod.

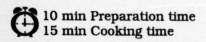 10 min Preparation time
15 min Cooking time

COD IN WHITE WINE

ingredients	Metric	Imperial	American
Packet parsley sauce mix	300 ml	½ pt	1¼ cup
Wineglass white wine	1	1	1
Salt and pepper			
125g/4 oz cod portions	4	4	4
Tomatoes, sliced	2	2	2
Garnish:			
Lemon wedges			

method

1. Make up the sauce mix substituting 1 wineglass liquid for wine. Adjust seasoning if necessary.

2. Pour into a shallow pan and place the fish on top.

3. Lay slices of tomato on top of the fish. Cover and poach gently for 10-15 minutes. Serve on a bed of rice and garnish with lemon wedges.

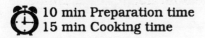 10 min Preparation time
15 min Cooking time

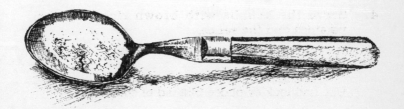

MACKEREL BAKED IN YOGHURT

ingredients	Metric	Imperial	American
Medium mackerel, cleaned	4	4	4
Natural yoghurt	150 ml	¼ pt	⅔ cup
Double (heavy) cream	4 tbsp	4 tbsp	4 tbsp
Salt and pepper			
Garnish:			
Lemon wedges			
Chopped fresh parsley			

method

1. Wash and dry the mackerel and place in a shallow dish.

2. Beat the yoghurt and cream together. Season to taste and pour over the fish.

3. Bake in a preheated oven at 190°C/375°F/Gas Mark 5 for 15-20 minutes until the fish is cooked through.

4. Serve garnished with lemon wedges and parsley.

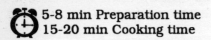 5-8 min Preparation time
15-20 min Cooking time

MACKEREL WITH MUSTARD SAUCE

ingredients	Metric	Imperial	American
Mackerel, cleaned	4	4	4
Butter	50 g	2 oz	¼ cup
Packet white sauce mix	300 ml	½ pt	1¼ cup
Ready made mustard	2 tsp	2 tsp	2 tsp
Salt and pepper			
Garnish:			
Chopped fresh parsley			

method

1. Wash and dry the mackerel. Make 3 small cuts diagonally across each side of the mackerel.

2. Brush with melted butter and grill (broil) or fry for about 6-8 minutes each side.

3. While cooking, make up the sauce mix according to the directions. Add the mustard and any remaining butter or juices to the sauce after the mackerel is cooked. Season.

4. Place the mackerel on a serving dish, pour the sauce over the top and sprinkle with chopped parsley. Serve with new potatoes and garden peas.

10 min Preparation time
15 min Cooking time

MACKEREL PROVENCALE

ingredients	Metric	Imperial	American
Mackerel, cleaned	4	4	4
Butter	25 g	1 oz	2 tbsp
Medium onion, chopped	1	1	1
Can chopped tomatoes	425 g	15 oz	15 oz
Bouquet garni	½ tsp	½ tsp	½ tsp
Salt and pepper			
Garnish:			
Watercress			

method

1. Wash and dry the mackerel. Diagonally score 3 times on each side of the body. Place on a grill tray.

2. Melt half of the butter and use to brush the mackerel. Grill (broil) on medium heat for about 6-8 minutes each side.

3. While the mackerel is cooking, make the sauce. Fry the onion in the remaining butter. Add the tomatoes and seasoning. Simmer until the mackerel is cooked.

4. Serve with the sauce poured over the fish and garnished with watercress.

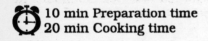 10 min Preparation time
20 min Cooking time

PRAWN AND TUNA RISOTTO

ingredients	Metric	Imperial	American
Butter	25 g	1 oz	2 tbsp
Large onion, chopped	1	1	1
Long-grain rice	175 g	6 oz	1 cup
Fish or vegetable stock	600 ml	1pt	2 ½ cups
Can tuna, drained and flaked	200 g	7 oz	7 oz
Prawns (shrimp), fresh, canned (drained) or frozen (thawed)	100 g	4 oz	⅔ cup
Can sweetcorn (corn kernels) and peppers, drained	200 g	7 oz	7 oz
Peas, cooked	100 g	4 oz	⅔ cup
Lemon juice	1 tbsp	1 tbsp	1 tbsp
Salt and pepper			
Packet parsley sauce mix	300 ml	½ pt	1 ¼ cup

method

1. Melt the butter in a pan and sauté the onion until soft. Add the rice and fry for a further 5 minutes, tossing well.

2. Add the stock, cover and cook for 15-20 minutes until the water is absorbed and rice is tender. (If using frozen peas, cook with the rice.)

3. Add the tuna, prawns, sweetcorn, peas, lemon juice and seasoning. Toss well and heat through gently.

4. Make up the parsley sauce mix according to directions and serve with the risotto.

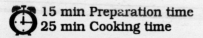 15 min Preparation time
25 min Cooking time

SALMON AND PRAWN PIE

ingredients	Metric	Imperial	American
Packet cheese sauce mix	300 ml	½ pt	1¼ cup
Can salmon, flaked	425 g	15 oz	15 oz
Prawns(shrimps), canned or frozen (thawed)	200 g	7 oz	7 oz
Peas, cooked	200 g	7 oz	1¼ cups
Made up mustard	1 tsp	1 tsp	1 tsp
Lemon juice	1 tsp	1 tsp	1 tsp
Hard-boiled (hard cooked) eggs, chopped	4	4	4
Mashed potato, instant or fresh	450 g	1 lb	2 cups

method

1. Make up the cheese sauce mix according to directions.

2. Add the salmon, shrimps, peas, mustard, lemon juice and eggs. Heat through and adjust the seasoning if necessary.

3. Turn into a flameproof pie dish and spread the mashed potato over the fish mixture. Fork up to make a pattern.

5. Flash under a hot grill (broiler) or place in a hot oven to brown the surface. Serve with a salad or vegetables.

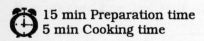 15 min Preparation time
5 min Cooking time

SEAFOOD PILAFF

ingredients	Metric	Imperial	American
Butter	25 g	1 oz	2 tbsp
Medium onion, chopped	1	1	1
Long-grain rice	225 g	8 oz	1 ¼ cups
Fish stock	600 ml	1 pt	2 ½ cups
Can crab meat or salmon	200 g	7 oz	7 oz
Prawns (shrimps)	200 g	7 oz	7 oz
Can pimentos, chopped	200 g	7 oz	7 oz
Peas	100 g	4 oz	¾ cup
Salt and pepper			
Garnish:			
Lemon wedges			
Chopped fresh parsley			

method

1. Melt the butter in a pan and sauté the onion until golden. Add the rice and toss for 2 minutes. (If using frozen peas add at this stage.)

2. Add the stock, cover and simmer for 15 minutes until the liquid is absorbed and rice is tender.

3. Add the crab, prawns, pimentos and peas. Adjust seasoning. Stir well and heat through. Serve garnished with lemon wedges and chopped parsley.

5-10 min Preparation time
25 min Cooking time

SMOKED HADDOCK BAKE

ingredients	Metric	Imperial	American
Cheddar cheese, grated	175 g	6 oz	1 ½ cups
Mashed potato, fresh or instant	350 g	12 oz	1 ½ cups
Eggs	4	4	4
Milk	150 ml	¼ pt	⅔ cup
Breadcrumbs or stuffing mix	50 g	2 oz	1 cup
Salt and pepper			
Butter	25 g	1 oz	2 tbsp
Smoked haddock, cooked and flaked	350 g	12 oz	12 oz
Garnish:			
Sliced tomato			
Parsley sprigs			

method

1. Mix half of the cheese with the potato. Pipe a fish shape on a serving dish, building up a deep border until all the potato is used. Alternatively, fork or pipe an edge in a serving dish.

2. Beat the eggs and brush the top of the potato. Bake in the oven at 200°C/400°F/Gas Mark 6 for about 15-20 minutes until browned.

3. While browning, add the milk, breadcrumbs, remaining cheese and seasoning to the eggs.

4. Melt the butter, pour in the egg mixture and stir until almost scrambled. Stir in the fish, heat through and pile into the centre of the browned potato.

5. Garnish and serve with peas and carrots.

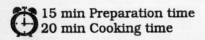 15 min Preparation time
20 min Cooking time

42

SMOKED SALMON ROLLS

ingredients	Metric	Imperial	American
Smoked mackerel, flesh only, flaked	100 g	4 oz	4 oz
Cream cheese	125 g	4 oz	½ cup
Mayonnaise	4 tbsp	4 tbsp	4 tbsp
Squeeze of lemon juice			
Salt and pepper			
Smoked salmon	225 g	8 oz	8 oz
Garnish:			
Lemon wedge			
Watercress			

method

1. Place the flaked mackerel, cream cheese, mayonnaise, lemon juice and seasoning in a bowl. Mix well until smooth.

2. Cut the slices of salmon into 8 strips. Place a portion of filling at one end of each and roll up.

3. Chill and serve garnished with a lemon wedge and watercress. These smoked salmon rolls may be served as a generous starter or as a main course with salad.

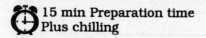 15 min Preparation time
Plus chilling

SPICED SEAFOOD PASTA

ingredients	Metric	Imperial	American
Butter	25 g	1 oz	2 tbsp
Medium onion, chopped	1	1	1
Can chopped tomatoes	425 g	15 oz	15 oz
Mixed herbs	½ tsp	½ tsp	½ tsp
Chilli powder	½ tsp	½ tsp	½ tsp
Ribbon noodles	450 g	1 lb	1 lb
Can shrimps or prawns, drained	200 g	7 oz	7 oz
Jar mussels in tomato sauce	100 g	4 oz	4 oz
Can anchovies, chopped	50 g	2 oz	2 oz
Black pepper			
Garnish:			
Chopped fresh parsley			

method

1. Melt the butter in a pan and sauté the onion until browned.

2. Add the tomatoes, herbs and chilli powder. Cover and simmer for 15-20 minutes.

3. While the sauce is simmering, cook the noodles in salted water for 10-15 minutes.

4. Add the shrimps, mussels and anchovies to the sauce. Season with black pepper and heat through.

5. Drain the noodles and place in a serving dish. Pour the sauce over the top and garnish with parsley.

10 min Preparation time
25 min Cooking time

THATCHED COD BAKE

ingredients	Metric	Imperial	American
Cod, skinned	450 g	1 lb	1 lb
Packet parsley sauce mix	300 ml	½ pt	1¼ cups
Squeeze of lemon juice			
Salt and pepper			
Tomatoes, sliced	4	4	4
Mashed potatoes, instant or fresh	675 g	1 ½ lb	3 cups
Cheddar cheese, grated	50 g	2 oz	½ cup

method

1. Dice the cod into 2.5 cm/1 inch cubes and place in a shallow 1 litre/2 pint/5 cup ovenproof dish.

2. Make up the sauce mix according to directions, add the lemon juice and adjust seasoning.

3. Pour over the cod and cover with sliced tomatoes. Pipe or spread the potato over the top and sprinkle with the cheese.

4. Bake in the oven at 190°C/375°F/Gas Mark 5 for 30 minutes until the topping is golden. Serve with garden peas.

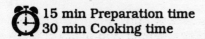
15 min Preparation time
30 min Cooking time

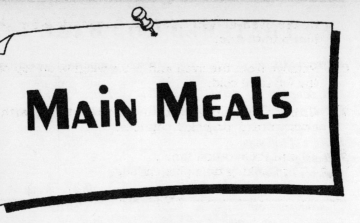

MAIN MEALS

BACON AND CHEESE LOAF

ingredients	Metric	Imperial	American
Packet stuffing mix	175 g	6 oz	6 oz
Streaky bacon rashers (slices), rinded	225 g	8 oz	8 oz
Cheddar cheese, grated	175 g	6 oz	1½ cups
Lean bacon, minced (ground)	450 g	1 lb	2 cups
Eggs, size 3, beaten	2	2	2

method

1. Make up the stuffing mix according to directions. Cool.

2. Stretch out the streaky bacon with the back of a knife and line a 900g/2 lb loaf tin (pan).

3. Add the cheese, minced bacon and eggs to the cooled stuffing and mix well.

4. Fill the loaf tin, level the top and cover with foil.

5. Place in a roasting tin (pan) half full of water. Bake

in the oven at 190°C/375°F/Gas Mark 5 for 1¼ hours until firm.

6. Remove from the oven and place weights on top of the foil until cold.

7. Chill in the refrigerator overnight. Serve with crusty bread or jacket potatoes.

⏰ 15 min Preparation time
1¾ hr Cooking time plus chilling

BARBECUE BREAST OF LAMB

ingredients	Metric	Imperial	American
Breast of lamb on the bone	*1.5 kg*	*3 lb*	*3 lb*
Tomato ketchup	*150 ml*	*¼ pt*	*⅔ cup*
Clear honey	*2 tbsp*	*2 tbsp*	*2 tbsp*
Worcestershire sauce	*2 tbsp*	*2 tbsp*	*2 tbsp*
Grated rind and juice of 1 orange			
Salt and pepper			

method

1. Cut the lamb into separate ribs and place in a roasting tin (pan).

2. Mix the remaining ingredients together and pour over the lamb.

3. Cover and cook in the oven at 180°C/350°F/Gas Mark 4 for 1½-2 hours, basting and turning occasionally in the sauce. Serve with plain or fried rice.

⏰ 5-10 min Preparation time
1½ -2 hr Cooking time

BARBECUE SPARE RIBS

ingredients	Metric	Imperial	American
Pork spare ribs, cut	1.5 kg	3 lb	3 lb
Marinade:			
Soy sauce	3 tbsp	3 tbsp	3 tbsp
Bottled spicy sauce	2 tbsp	2 tbsp	3 tbsp
Worcestershire sauce	1 tbsp	1 tbsp	1 tbsp
Tomato ketchup	1 tbsp	1 tbsp	1 tbsp
Coarse cut marmalade	1 tbsp	1 tbsp	1 tbsp

method

1. Place all the marinade ingredients in a saucepan. Heat gently, stirring until blended. Leave to cool.

2. Toss the ribs in the marinade. Cover and place in the refrigerator overnight if possible. Turn the ribs occasionally.

3. Place the ribs in a roasting tin (pan). Cover and cook in the oven at 200°C/400°F/Gas Mark 6 for 1-1¼ hours, turning twice during cooking. Serve on a bed of rice.

5-10 min Preparation time
        Plus marinating
1 -1¼ hr Cooking time

BEEF BORDEAUX

ingredients	Metric	Imperial	American
Butter	25 g	1 oz	2 tbsp
Braising steaks, 100 g/4 oz each	4	4	4
Bunch spring onions (scallions), chopped	1	1	1
Chopped fresh parsley	2 tbsp	2 tbsp	2 tbsp
Red wine	150 ml	¼ pt	⅔ cup
Rich gravy	150 ml	¼ pt	⅔ cup
Salt and pepper			
Can chopped mushrooms, drained	300 g	10 oz	10 oz

method

1. Melt the butter and fry the steaks quickly on both sides to seal. Transfer to a casserole.

2. Place the remaining ingredients, except the mushrooms, in a pan and bring to the boil.

3. Pour over the steaks. Cover and cook in the oven at 170°C/325°F/Gas Mark 3 for 1¼ hours.

4. Add the mushrooms and cook for a further 15 minutes. Serve with potatoes and a green vegetable or carrots.

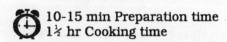
10-15 min Preparation time
1¼ hr Cooking time

BEEF OLIVES PROVENCALE

ingredients	Metric	Imperial	American
Slices topside (top round), 50g/2 oz each	8	8	8
Streaky bacon rashers (slices), rinded	4	4	4
Thick beef sausages	4	4	4
Butter	25 g	1 oz	2 tbsp
Jar red and green pepper or mushroom sauce	450 g	1 lb	1 lb
Glass red wine	1	1	1
Garnish:			
Chopped fresh parsley			

method

1. Place each piece of meat between wetted grease-proof (waxed) paper and bat out until thin with a rolling pin.

2. Wrap the bacon spirally around each sausage and place at one end of meat. Roll up and secure with a cocktail stick (toothpick) or tie with string.

3. Melt the butter and fry the beef olives quickly to seal in the juices. Transfer to a casserole.

4. Heat the jar of sauce with the wine and pour over the beef olives.

5. Cover and cook in the oven at 190°C/375°F/Gas Mark 5 for 1-1¼ hours.

6. Remove the cocktail stick or string and serve on a bed of rice or noodles garnished with parsley. Accompany with French beans and sweetcorn.

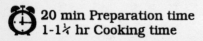
20 min Preparation time
1-1¼ hr Cooking time

BEEF WITH PINEAPPLE AND BLACK BEAN SAUCE

ingredients	Metric	Imperial	American
Butter	50 g	2 oz	¼ cup
Medium onion, chopped	1	1	1
Fillet (filet mignon) or rump steak, cut into 2.5 cm/1 inch cubes	450 g	1 lb	1 lb
Jar black bean sauce	450 g	1 lb	1 lb
Can baby sweetcorn, drained	350 g	12 oz	12 oz
Can pineapple pieces, drained	200 g	7 oz	7 oz
Salt and pepper			

method

1. Melt the butter in a pan and gently fry the onion and steak for about 5-8 minutes until browned.

2. Add the black bean sauce and sweetcorn, cover and simmer for 10 minutes.

3. Add the pineapple and heat through. Season. Serve with crisp fried stir fry.

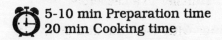
5-10 min Preparation time
20 min Cooking time

BEEF AND TOMATO HERBED COBBLER

ingredients	Metric	Imperial	American
Stewing steak, diced	450 g	1 lb	1 lb
Flour	25 g	1 oz	¼ cup
Butter	50 g	2 oz	¼ cup
Large onion, sliced	1	1	1
Can plum tomatoes	425 g	15 oz	15 oz
Can condensed tomato soup	425 g	15 oz	15 oz
Salt and pepper			
Mixed herbs	1 tsp	1 tsp	1 tsp
Packet scone (biscuit) mix	225 g	8 oz	8 oz
Little milk to glaze			

method

1. Toss the meat in the flour. Melt the butter and fry the meat and onion until browned.

2. Add the tomatoes and soup and bring to the boil. Season to taste and transfer to a casserole dish.

3. Cover and cook in the oven at 150°C/300°F/Gas Mark 2 for 2 ½-3 hours until the meat is tender.

4. Add the herbs to the dry scone mix and make up according to directions. Cut into 8-10 rounds with a 5 cm/2 inch biscuit (cookie) cutter.

5. Place on top of the beef and brush with milk. Bake at 220°C/425°F/Gas Mark 7 for the last 10-15 minutes of cooking time until the scones are risen and browned. Serve with creamed potatoes and a green vegetable.

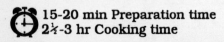

15-20 min Preparation time
2½-3 hr Cooking time

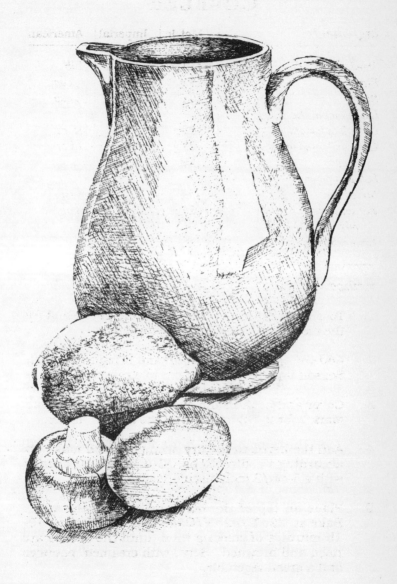

BUCKING BRONCO STEAK

ingredients	Metric	Imperial	American
Fillet (filet mignon) steaks, about 175g/6 oz each, sliced 2cm/¾ inch thick	4	4	4
Salt and pepper			
Butter	50 g	2 oz	¼ cup
Cloves garlic, crushed	2	2	2
Medium onion, finely chopped	1	1	1
Milk	150 ml	¼ pt	⅔ cup
Worcestershire sauce	2 tbsp	2 tbsp	2 tbsp
Brandy	2 tbsp	2 tbsp	2 tbsp
Cornflour (cornstarch)	2 tsp	2 tsp	2 tsp
Squeeze of lemon juice			
Can sliced mushrooms, drained	175 g	6 oz	6 oz
Single (light) cream	150 ml	¼ pt	⅔ cup
Chopped fresh parsley	1 tsp	1 tsp	1 tsp

method

1. Season the steaks. Melt 25g/1 oz/2 tbsp of the butter and fry the seasoned steaks and garlic to your liking. Remove and keep warm.

2. Melt the remaining butter and fry the onion until browned.

3. Add most of the milk, the Worcestershire sauce and brandy and bring to the boil.

4. Blend the cornflour with a little of the reserved milk, add to the pan and stir until slightly thickened.

54

5. Reduce the heat, add the lemon juice, mushrooms, cream and parsley and stir until simmering. Pour over the steaks. Serve with sauté or chipped potatoes, grilled (broiled) tomatoes and a green vegetable.

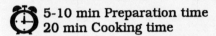 5-10 min Preparation time
20 min Cooking time

CHICKEN ALMONDINE

ingredients	Metric	Imperial	American
Butter	25 g	1 oz	2 tbsp
Medium chicken portions or 8 drumsticks	4	4	4
425g/15 oz cans cream of chicken soup	2	2	2
Salt and pepper			
Flaked almonds	50 g	2 oz	½ cup
Garnish:			
A few flaked toasted almonds			
Chopped fresh parsley			

method

1. Melt the butter in a pan and fry the chicken portions on both sides until browned.

2. Pour over the chicken soup, season, sprinkle with the nuts (reserving a few for garnish). Bring to the boil. Cover and simmer gently for about 30 minutes until the chicken is tender.

3. Garnish with toasted almonds and parsley. Serve with boiled rice or noodles and a green vegetable.

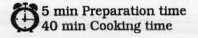 5 min Preparation time
40 min Cooking time

CHICKEN WITH BASIL AND TOMATOES

ingredients	Metric	Imperial	American
Medium chicken breasts, boned	4	4	4
Flour	25 g	1 oz	¼ cup
Butter	25 g	1 oz	2 tbsp
Medium onion, chopped	1	1	1
Can chopped tomatoes	425 g	15 oz	15 oz
Basil	2 tsp	2 tsp	2 tsp
Salt and pepper			

method

1. Toss the chicken in the flour. Melt the butter and brown the chicken and onion.

2. Add the tomatoes, basil and seasoning.

3. Cover and simmer gently for 30 minutes until the chicken is tender. Serve with rice or new potatoes and vegetables.

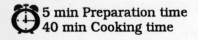
5 min Preparation time
40 min Cooking time

CHICKEN MARYLAND PIE

ingredients	Metric	Imperial	American
Packet white sauce mix	30 g	½ pt	1¼ cups
Cooked chicken, diced	350 g	12 oz	2 cups
Can sweetcorn (corn kernels) and peppers, drained	350 g	12 oz	12 oz
Bananas, sliced	2	2	2
Salt and pepper			
Puff pastry	225 g	8 oz	8 oz
A little milk to glaze			

method

1. Make up the sauce mix according to the directions. Add the chicken, sweetcorn and peppers and bananas. Fold in well to coat with the sauce, season and place in a pie dish.

2. Roll out the pastry, cover the chicken mixture and brush with milk.

3. Bake in the oven at 200°C/400°F/Gas Mark 6 for 30-40 minutes until golden brown.

15 min Preparation time
30-40 min Cooking time

CHICKEN WITH PEPPERED RICE

ingredients	Metric	Imperial	American
Butter	50 g	2 oz	¼ cup
Chicken portions	4	4	4
Chicken stock	600 ml	1 pt	2 ½ cups
Long grain rice	225 g	8 oz	1 ¼ cups
Red and green pepper, chopped	125 g	4 oz	1 cup
Large onion, chopped	1	1	1
Tomato purée (paste)	1 tbsp	1 tbsp	1 tbsp
Paprika pepper	½ tsp	½ tsp	½ tsp
Pinch of mixed herbs			
Salt and pepper			

method

1. Melt the butter in a pan and fry the chicken until browned on both sides. Add 300ml/½ pint/1¼ cups of the stock, cover and simmer for 15 minutes.

2. Add the remainder of the stock, the rice, pepper, onion, tomato purée, paprika, herbs and seasoning. Mix well.

3. Cover and simmer for a further 15-20 minutes until the rice is cooked and the liquid absorbed. Serve with broccoli and sweetcorn.

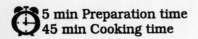 5 min Preparation time
45 min Cooking time

CHICKEN PIMENTO

ingredients	Metric	Imperial	American
Butter	25 g	1 oz	2 tbsp
Medium chicken breasts, skinned	4	4	4
Can pimentos, drained and cut into slices	200 g	7 oz	7 oz
Cheddar cheese, grated	125 g	4 oz	1 cup
Single (light) cream	150 ml	¼ pt	⅔ cup
Milk	150 ml	¼ pt	⅔ cup
Salt and pepper			
Garnish:			
Chopped fresh parsley			

method

1. Melt the butter in a pan and fry the chicken for 15-20 minutes, turning halfway through cooking.

2. Place the pimentos, cheese, cream and milk in a saucepan and stir until combined. Heat gently until just beginning to simmer.

3. Place the chicken on a plate with the sauce poured over and a sprinkling of parsley. Serve with jacket potatoes or rice and a green vegetable.

10 min Preparation time
20 min Cooking time

CHICKEN AND SWEETCORN A LA CREME

ingredients	Metric	Imperial	American
Butter	25 g	1 oz	2 tbsp
Medium onion, sliced	1	1	1
Cooked chicken, cut into strips	350 g	12 oz	2 cups
Dry white wine	150 ml	¼ pt	⅔ cup
Salt and pepper			
Double (heavy) cream	150 ml	¼ pt	⅔ cup
Can sweetcorn (corn kernels), drained	175 g	6 oz	6 oz
Can pimentos, drained and sliced	200 g	7 oz	7 oz

method

1. Melt the butter in a pan and sauté the onion until golden brown. Add the chicken, wine and seasoning. Bring to the boil.

2. Add the cream, sweetcorn and pimentos. Heat through and serve with rice and a green vegetable.

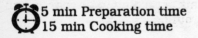 5 min Preparation time
15 min Cooking time

CHILLI COBBLER

ingredients	Metric	Imperial	American
Minced (ground) beef	350 g	12 oz	1½ cups
Medium onion, chopped	1	1	1
Chilli powder	2 tsp	2 tsp	2 tsp
Can chopped tomatoes	425 g	15 oz	15 oz
Salt and pepper			
Can red kidney beans, drained	425 g	15 oz	15 oz
Packet scone (biscuit) mix	225 g	8 oz	8 oz
Milk to glaze			

method

1. Heat the pan and fry the mince, onion and chilli powder together until lightly browned.

2. Add the tomatoes and seasoning and simmer for 20 minutes.

3. Stir in the kidney beans, heat through, then transfer into a 600ml/1 pint/2½ cup dish.

4. Make up the scone mix according to directions and cut out 5cm/2 inch rounds.

5. Place the scones, overlapping, around the edge, then brush them with a little milk. Bake in the oven at 200°C/400°F/Gas Mark 6 for 10-15 minutes until the topping is risen and golden. Serve with rice or whole buttered sweetcorn cobs.

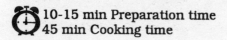 10-15 min Preparation time
45 min Cooking time

CHILLI MINCE

ingredients	Metric	Imperial	American
Minced (ground) beef	450 g	1 lb	1 lb
Onion, chopped	1	1	1
Can red kidney beans, drained	425 g	15 oz	15 oz
Can baked beans	200 g	7 oz	7 oz
Chilli powder	3 tsp	3 tsp	3 tsp
Salt and pepper			
Beef stock	150 ml	¼ pt	⅔ cup
Cornflour (cornstarch)	1 tbsp	1 tbsp	1 tbsp
Cold water	2 tbsp	2 tbsp	2 tbsp

method

1. Heat the pan and fry the mince and onion, stirring well until lightly browned. Stir in all the remaining ingredients, except the cornflour and water.

2. Bring to the boil, cover and simmer for 30 minutes.

3. Blend the cornflour and water together. Add to the mince and cook until thickened. Serve with jacket potatoes or French bread and green salad.

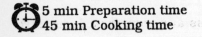
5 min Preparation time
45 min Cooking time

CHILLI STUFFED TACOS

ingredients	Metric	Imperial	American
Butter	25 g	1oz	2 tbsp
Minced (ground) beef	450 g	1lb	2 cups
Large onion, chopped	1	1	1
Green pepper, chopped	1	1	1
Garlic purée (optional)	½ tsp	½ tsp	½ tsp
Chilli powder or to taste	1-2 tsp	1-2 tsp	1-2 tsp
Mixed herbs	1 tsp	1 tsp	1 tsp
Can chopped tomatoes	425 g	15 oz	15 oz
Salt and pepper			
Tomato purée (paste)	4 tbsp	4 tbsp	4 tbsp
Can red kidney beans, drained	425 g	15 oz	15 oz
Taco shells	8	8	8
To serve:			
Sour cream	150 ml	¼ pt	⅔ cup
Shredded lettuce			
Grated Cheddar cheese			

method

1. Melt the butter in a pan and fry the beef, onion and pepper until browned. Add all the other chilli ingredients, except the kidney beans. Cover and simmer for 20 minutes, stirring occasionally.

2. Add the kidney beans and cook for a further 10 minutes.

3. Spoon the mixture into the taco shells and serve topped with sour cream, shredded lettuce and a sprinkling of cheese.

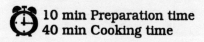 10 min Preparation time
40 min Cooking time

COUNTRY GARDEN CHICKEN FLAN

ingredients	Metric	Imperial	American
Packet stuffing mix (flavour of choice)	75 g	3 oz	3 oz
Egg	1	1	1
Butter, melted	50 g	2 oz	¼ cup
Packet white sauce mix	300 ml	½ pt	1¼ cups
Can sliced mushrooms, drained	200 g	7 oz	7 oz
Cooked chicken, diced	225 g	8 oz	1 ⅓ cups
Salt and pepper			

method

1. Make up the stuffing mix according to directions. Stir in the egg and melted butter. Leave to stand for 5-10 minutes.

2. Press the mixture into the base and sides of a 20cm/8 inch greased flan ring or dish. Bake blind in the oven at 190°C/375°F/Gas Mark 5 for 20 minutes.

3. While cooking, make up the white sauce mix. Add the mushrooms and chicken. Adjust seasoning and heat through thoroughly.

4. Pour the chicken mixture into the cooked flan case, heating through in the oven, if necessary. Serve with jacket potatoes and sweetcorn.

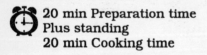 20 min Preparation time
Plus standing
20 min Cooking time

CRANBERRY AND ORANGE PORK CHOPS

ingredients	Metric	Imperial	American
Butter	25 g	1 oz	2 tbsp
Pork loin chops, 100 g/4 oz each	4	4	4
Jar cranberry and orange sauce	175 g	6 oz	6 oz
Red wine	150 ml	¼ pt	⅔ cup
Clear honey	4 tbsp	4 tbsp	4 tbsp
Black pepper			

method

1. Melt the butter in a pan and fry the chops for 2 minutes to seal the juices.

2. Remove from the pan and add the cranberry and orange sauce, wine and honey to the pan. Stir well and bring to a simmer. Season with pepper.

3. Replace the chops in the pan and coat with the sauce. Cover and simmer for 25-30 minutes until tender. Serve with boiled rice and vegetables.

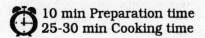 10 min Preparation time
25-30 min Cooking time

DEVILLED BEEF CASSEROLE

ingredients	Metric	Imperial	American
Stewing steak, cubed	675 g	1 ½ lb	1 ½ lb
Seasoned flour	2 tbsp	2 tbsp	2 tbsp
Butter	50 g	2 oz	¼ cup
Large onions, sliced	2	2	2
Beef stock	600 ml	1 pt	2 ½ cups
Worcestershire sauce	2 tbsp	2 tbsp	2 tbsp
Mustard	1 tsp	1 tsp	1 tsp
Carrots, cut into 2.5cm/1 inch pieces	225 g	8 oz	2 cups
Turnips, cut into 2.5cm/1 inch pieces or parsnips (rutabaga), cut into wedges	225 g	8 oz	2 cups
Salt and pepper			

method

1. Place the meat in a bag and toss in the seasoned flour.

2. Melt the butter and fry the onions until opaque. Add the meat, tossing well until browned.

3. Add all the remaining ingredients, stir and bring to the boil.

4. Transfer to a casserole. Cover and cook in the oven at 170°C/325°F/Gas Mark 3 for 2-2 ½ hours until tender. Alternatively, simmer gently on top of the cooker, stirring occasionally, until tender.

5. Serve with jacket potatoes, boiled rice or noodles and a green vegetable.

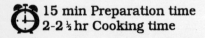 15 min Preparation time
2-2 ½ hr Cooking time

DEVILLED DRUMSTICKS

ingredients	Metric	Imperial	American
Chicken drumsticks, cooked, or 4 chicken portions, cooked	8	8	8
Dried breadcrumbs	50 g	2 oz	1 cup
Butter, melted	50 g	2 oz	¼ cup
Devil Paste:			
French mustard	6 tsp	6 tsp	6 tsp
Worcestershire sauce	2 tsp	2 tsp	2 tsp
Paprika pepper	2 tsp	2 tsp	2 tsp
Curry powder	1 tbsp	1 tbsp	1 tbsp
Tomato purée (paste)	2 tbsp	2 tbsp	2 tbsp
Softened butter	50 g	2 oz	¼ cup

method

1. Mix all the paste ingredients together until blended.

2. Skin the chicken and make a few small cuts into the meat.

3. Push the paste into the cuts and spread the remainder over the meat.

4. Coat the meat with breadcrumbs, place on a grill (broiler) rack and brush with melted butter.

5. Grill (broil) over a medium heat until golden and heated through. Alternatively, place on a baking sheet and cook in the oven at 175-200°C/375-400°F/Gas Mark 5-6 until heated through, crisp and golden. Serve with salads and French bread.

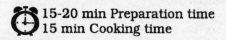 15-20 min Preparation time
15 min Cooking time

FILLET STEAK EN CROUTE

ingredients	Metric	Imperial	American
Butter	25 g	1 oz	2 tbsp
Fillet (filet mignon) steaks, 175g/6 oz each	4	4	4
Packet prepared puff pastry	450 g	1 lb	1 lb
Garlic purée	2 tsp	2 tsp	2 tsp
Smooth pâté with herbs	100 g	4 oz	½ cup
Egg, beaten	1	1	1
Garnish:			
Watercress			

method

1. Spread the butter on both sides of the steaks and place in a roasting tin (pan).

2. Cook in the oven at 220°C/425°F/Gas Mark 7 for 5 minutes. Cool.

3. Divide the pastry into 4 and roll out each piece large enough to enclose the steak.

4. Place a piece of steak in the centre of the pastry, spread with garlic purée and then pâté.

5. Brush the pastry edges with beaten egg and bring together to form a parcel. Place on a wetted baking sheet, join side down, and chill for 30 minutes.

6. Brush the pastry top with egg. Bake in the oven at 220°C/425°F/Gas Mark 7 for 20-25 minutes until the pastry is golden brown. Garnish with watercress and serve with hot vegetables or a green salad.

20 min Preparation time plus chilling
25-30 min Cooking time

GAMMON STEAKS WITH MUSTARD SAUCE

ingredients	Metric	Imperial	American
Gammon or (smoked) ham steaks, 100 g/ 4 oz each	4	4	4
Packet white sauce mix	300 ml	½ pt	1¼ cups
Wholegrain mustard	1 tbsp	1 tbsp	1 tbsp

method

1. Grill (broil) the gammon steaks. While cooking, make up the sauce mix according to directions.

2. Add the mustard to the sauce and cook for 1 minute.

3. Pour the mustard sauce over the steaks. Serve with rice or potatoes and a green vegetable.

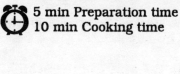 5 min Preparation time
10 min Cooking time

GAMMON STEAKS WITH PARSLEY AND MUSHROOM SAUCE

ingredients	Metric	Imperial	American
Gammon or (smoked) ham steaks	4	4	4
Packet parsley sauce mix	300 ml	½ pt	1¼ cups
Can sliced mushrooms, drained	200 g	7 oz	7 oz

method

1. Grill (broil) the gammon steaks. While cooking, make up the sauce mix according to directions.

2. Add the mushrooms to the sauce and heat through.

3. Pour the sauce over the steaks. Serve with grilled (broiled) tomatoes and jacket potatoes.

5 min Preparation time
10 min Cooking time

HAM AND MUSHROOM TAGLIATELLE

ingredients	Metric	Imperial	American
Tagliatelle	225 g	8 oz	8 oz
300 ml/½ pt/1¼ cup packets white sauce mix	2	2	2
Cooked ham or bacon, sliced	225 g	8 oz	8 oz
Can sliced mushrooms, drained	200 g	7 oz	7 oz
Salt and pepper			
Cheddar cheese, grated	125 g	4 oz	1 cup
Garnish:			
Chopped fresh parsley			

method

1. Cook the tagliatelle in a pan of boiling salted water. While cooking, make up the sauce mix according to directions.

2. Add the ham and mushrooms to the sauce. Adjust seasoning.

3. Drain the tagliatelle. Add the cheese and toss well. Serve on a platter, topped with the sauce mixture. Garnish with parsley.

variation

Use chicken in place of ham or a mixture of both.

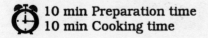
10 min Preparation time
10 min Cooking time

71

HUNTERS PIE

ingredients	Metric	Imperial	American
Cold cooked beef, lamb or pork	450 g	1 lb	1 lb
Large onion	1	1	1
Can chopped tomatoes	425 g	15 oz	15 oz
Can baked beans	425 g	15 oz	15 oz
Flour	2 tsp	2 tsp	2 tsp
Gravy powder	2 tsp	2 tsp	2 tsp
Pinch of mixed herbs			
Salt and pepper			
Potatoes, thinly sliced	450 g	1 lb	1 lb
Cheddar cheese, grated	50 g	2 oz	½ cup

method

1. Mince or chop the meat and onion in a food processor.

2. Place in a bowl and stir in tomatoes, baked beans, flour, gravy powder, herbs and seasoning.

3. Turn the mixture into a pie dish and arrange the potatoes on top, overlapping, but in a single layer.

4. Bake in the oven at 190°C/375°F/Gas Mark 5 for 40-50 minutes. Sprinkle with the grated cheese 10 minutes before the end of the cooking time. Serve with a green vegetable.

10-15 min Preparation time
40-50 min Cooking time

ITALIAN LIVER

ingredients	Metric	Imperial	American
Lamb's liver, cut into 1cm/½ inch strips	450 g	1 lb	1 lb
Milk	300 ml	½ pt	1¼ cups
Flour	25 g	1 oz	¼ cup
Butter	25 g	1 oz	2 tbsp
Onions, sliced	450 g	1 lb	1 lb
Stock	150 ml	¼ pt	⅔ cup
Tomato purée (paste)	2 tbsp	2 tbsp	2 tbsp
Large pinch of mixed herbs			
Salt and pepper			
Garnish:			
Single (light) cream	2 tbsp	2 tbsp	2 tbsp
Chopped fresh parsley			

method

1. Soak the liver in the milk for 1 hour if possible. Drain, reserving the milk, and coat in the flour.

2. Melt the butter and brown the liver quickly, tossing well. Remove from the pan and fry the onions until tender.

3. Add the milk, stock, tomato purée, herbs, seasoning and liver. Stir well.

4. Bring to the boil, cover and simmer gently for 10-15 minutes until the liver is tender.

5. Place in a serving dish, swirl the cream in the centre and garnish with parsley. Serve with rice and a green vegetable.

10 min Preparation time plus soaking
25 min Cooking time

73

ITALIAN MEATBALLS

ingredients	Metric	Imperial	American
Minced (ground) beef	450 g	1 lb	1 lb
Packet stuffing mix	25 g	1 oz	⅓ cup
Garlic purée	1 tsp	1 tsp	1 tsp
Parmesan cheese	2 tbsp	2 tbsp	2 tbsp
Flour	2 tbsp	2 tbsp	2 tbsp
Butter	25 g	1 oz	2 tbsp
Jar of red and green pepper sauce	450 g	1 lb	1 lb
Garnish:			
Chopped fresh parsley			

method

1. Place the minced beef, stuffing mix, garlic purée and Parmesan cheese in a bowl. Mix well, shape into 2.5cm/1 inch balls and toss in flour.

2. Melt the butter and fry the meatballs until browned.

3. Stir in the pepper sauce, cover and simmer for 20 minutes, stirring twice during cooking. Serve on a bed of spaghetti or macaroni and garnish with parsley.

variation

To enhance the sauce, 2 tablespoons red wine may be added during cooking.

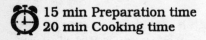
15 min Preparation time
20 min Cooking time

KIDNEY STROGANOFF

ingredients	Metric	Imperial	American
Butter	25 g	1 oz	2 tbsp
Onion, finely chopped	1	1	1
Lamb's kidneys, skinned, cored and quartered	12	12	12
Flour	25 g	1 oz	¼ cup
Milk	300 ml	½ pt	1¼ cups
Salt and pepper			
Can sliced mushrooms, drained	200 g	7 oz	7 oz
Sour cream or natural yoghurt	150 ml	¼ pt	⅔ cup
Garnish:			
Chopped fresh parsley			

method

1. Melt the butter in a pan and sauté the onion for 2 minutes.

2. Toss the kidneys in the flour and add to the pan. Cook for 4-5 minutes, tossing well until the kidneys are browned.

3. Add the milk slowly, stirring well to make a smooth sauce. Season and add the mushrooms.

4. Cover and simmer for 15-20 minutes until the kidneys are tender.

5. Swirl in the sour cream or yoghurt. Reheat without boiling.

6. Place in a serving dish and garnish with parsley. Serve with rice and grilled (broiled) or braised tomatoes.

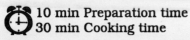

10 min Preparation time
30 min Cooking time

LAMB KEBABS

ingredients	Metric	Imperial	American
Boneless leg of lamb	450 g	1 lb	1 lb
Green pepper	1	1	1
Red pepper	1	1	1
Medium onions	2	2	2
Marinade:			
Oil	4 tbsp	4 tbsp	4 tbsp
Worcestershire sauce	2 tbsp	2 tbsp	2 tbsp
Lemon juice	2 tbsp	2 tbsp	2 tbsp
Salt and pepper			

method

1. Cut the lamb, peppers and onions into 2.5cm/ 1 inch cubes and thread alternately onto 8 skewers. Place in a shallow dish.

2. Mix the marinade ingredients together and pour over the kebabs. Cover and leave for at least 1 hour, turning occasionally.

3. Cook the kebabs under a medium grill (broiler) or on a barbecue for 10-15 minutes, turning frequently and basting with the marinade. Serve with salad and crusty garlic bread.

10 min Preparation time
plus marinating
10-15 min Cooking time

Leek and Ham au Gratin

ingredients	Metric	Imperial	American
Slices ham	8	8	8
Large prepared and cooked leeks or small canned celery hearts, drained	8	8	8
Packet cheese sauce mix	300 ml	½ pt	1¼ cup
Cheddar cheese, grated	50 g	2 oz	½ cup
Garnish:			
Tomatoes, sliced	2	2	2
Chopped fresh parsley			

method

1. Roll a slice of ham around each leek or celery heart and place in a shallow dish.

2. Make up the sauce mix according to directions and pour over the ham parcels. Sprinkle with the grated cheese.

3. Bake in the oven at 190°C/375°F/Gas Mark 5 for 30 minutes until the top is golden brown. Serve garnished with sliced tomato and a sprinkling of parsley.

10 min Preparation time
30 min Cooking time

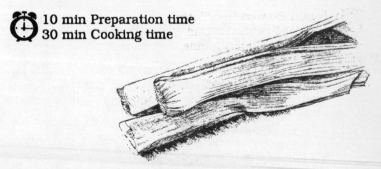

LIVER SAUSAGE QUICHE

ingredients	Metric	Imperial	American
Margarine	15 g	½ oz	1 tbsp
Medium onion, chopped	1	1	1
Streaky bacon rashers (slices), chopped	2	2	2
Baked pastry flan case (pie shell)	20 cm	8 inch	8 inch
Smooth liver sausage, thinly sliced	75 g	3 oz	½ cup
Eggs, size 3	2	2	2
Milk	300 ml	½ pt	1 ¼ cups
Salt and pepper			
Pinch of mixed herbs			
Cheddar cheese, grated	50 g	2 oz	½ cup
Garnish:			
Tomato slices			

method

1. Heat the margarine in a pan and sauté the onion and bacon for 2-3 minutes until lightly browned.

2. Place the pastry case on a baking tray. Sprinkle over the bacon and onion mixture and liver sausage slices.

3. Beat the eggs, milk, seasoning, herbs and cheese together and pour into the pastry case.

4. Bake in the oven at 190°C/375°F/Gas Mark 5 for about 45 minutes until set and golden brown. Garnish with sliced tomato and serve hot or cold.

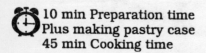 10 min Preparation time
Plus making pastry case
45 min Cooking time

MEAT LOAF

ingredients	Metric	Imperial	American
Packet stuffing mix	175 g	6 oz	6 oz
Minced (ground) beef	450 g	1 lb	1 lb
Sausagemeat	100 g	4 oz	½ cup
Medium onion, chopped	1	1	1
Red or green pepper, chopped	1	1	1
Worcestershire sauce	1 tbsp	1 tbsp	1 tbsp
Tomato ketchup or purée (paste)	1 tbsp	1 tbsp	1 tbsp
Eggs, beaten	2	2	2
Salt and pepper			

method

1. Make up the stuffing mix according to the directions. Place all the ingredients in a bowl and mix well.

2. Spoon the mixture into a 450g/1 lb loaf tin (pan) and smooth the top. Bake in the oven at 190°C/375°F/Gas Mark 5 for 1-1¼ hours. Cover the top with foil if browning too much.

3. Leave to stand for a few minutes, then turn out and slice. Serve with tomato or mushroom sauce and hot vegetables.

4. The meat loaf may also be served cold with salad.

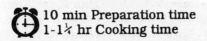 10 min Preparation time
1-1¼ hr Cooking time

MEAT AND POTATO LAYER

ingredients	Metric	Imperial	American
Butter	25 g	1 oz	2 tbsp
Medium onion, chopped	1	1	1
Cooked beef, pork or lamb, minced (ground)	350 g	12 oz	1½ cups
Tomato purée (paste)	3 tbsp	3 tbsp	3 tbsp
Worcestershire sauce	2 tsp	2 tsp	2 tsp
Large pinch of mixed herbs			
Salt and pepper			
Potatoes, boiled and sliced	450 g	1 lb	1 lb
Can chopped tomatoes	425 g	15 oz	15 oz
Egg	1	1	1
Flour	1½ tbsp	1½ tbsp	1½ tbsp
Natural yoghurt	150 g	5 oz	⅔ cup
Garnish:			
Paprika pepper			
Chopped fresh parsley			

method

1. Melt the butter in a pan and sauté the onion for 2 minutes. Remove from the heat and stir in the meat, tomato purée, Worcestershire sauce, herbs and seasoning.

2. Using half of the potatoes, arrange a layer in a casserole. Top with the meat mixture and spread the tomatoes over this.

3. Arrange another layer of potatoes to finish. Cover the casserole and bake in the oven at 190°C/375°F /Gas Mark 5 for 30 minutes.

4. Beat the egg and blend in the flour and yoghurt. Season and spread over the potato topping.

5. Bake without the cover for a further hour. Garnish with a sprinkling of paprika and parsley before serving.

variation

For a cheesy flavoured topping, use sour cream in place of yoghurt.

 15 min Preparation time
1½ hr Cooking time

MINTED LAMB CUTLETS

ingredients	Metric	Imperial	American
Lamb cutlets	*8*	*8*	*8*
Salt and pepper			
Mint jelly	*3 tbsp*	*3 tbsp*	*3 tbsp*

method

1. Season the cutlets and spread half of the mint jelly on one side.

2. Cook under a medium grill (broiler) for 7-8 minutes.

3. Turn over, spread with the remaining mint jelly and cook for a further 7-8 minutes. Serve with any juices, new potatoes and grilled (broiled) beefsteak tomatoes.

variation

Lamb loin chops or noisettes may also be used.

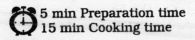 5 min Preparation time
15 min Cooking time

81

MOCK BEEF STROGANOFF

ingredients	Metric	Imperial	American
Butter	50 g	2 oz	¼ cup
Medium onion, chopped	1	1	1
Fillet (filet mignon) or rump steak, sliced into thin strips	450 g	1 lb	1 lb
Jar carbonara sauce	450 g	1 lb	1 lb
Can sliced mushrooms, drained	300 g	10 oz	10 oz
Salt and pepper			
Garnish:			
Chopped fresh parsley			

method

1. Melt half of the butter in a pan and sauté the onion until lightly browned.

2. Add the remaining butter and fry the meat for 4-5 minutes, tossing well.

3. Add the remaining ingredients, adjust seasoning and heat through.

4. Serve on a bed of rice or noodles, garnished with chopped parsley. Accompany with a green vegetable.

5-10 min Preparation time
15 min Cooking time

MUSTARD CRUMB PORK CHOPS

ingredients	Metric	Imperial	American
Parmesan cheese	5 oz	2 oz	½ cup
Dried breadcrumbs	25 g	1 oz	¼ cup
Prepared mustard of choice	1 tbsp	1 tbsp	1 tbsp
Loin pork chops, 100 g/4 oz each	4	4	4
Seasoned flour	1 tbsp	1 tbsp	1 tbsp
Egg, beaten	1	1	1
Butter	50 g	2 oz	¼ cup
Oil	2 tbsp	2 tbsp	2 tbsp
Garnish:			
Parsley sprigs			

method

1. Mix the cheese and breadcrumbs together.

2. Spread the mustard on both sides of the chops and coat in the flour.

3. Dip in the egg, then toss in the breadcrumb mixture.

4. Melt the butter and oil in a frying pan (skillet) and fry the chops for 20 minutes, turning occasionally until cooked through. Garnish with parsley sprigs and serve with new potatoes and a green vegetable.

10-12 min Preparation time
20 min Cooking time

MUSTANG PORK CHOPS

ingredients	Metric	Imperial	American
Grated rind and juice of 2 oranges			
Demerara sugar	3 tbsp	3 tbsp	3 tbsp
Whole grain mustard	1 tbsp	1 tbsp	1 tbsp
Salt and pepper			
Loin pork chops, 100 g/4 oz each	4	4	4
Garnish:			
Watercress			
Orange wedges			

method

1. Place the orange rind, juice, sugar and mustard in a pan and heat, stirring, until the sugar is dissolved.

2. Boil gently until the sauce becomes syrupy. Remove from the heat. Season.

3. Place the chops on a grill (broiler) pan. Baste at intervals until the chops are cooked. Place on a serving dish.

4. Reheat any remaining sauce and pour over the chops. Serve garnished with watercress and orange wedges.

10 min Preparation time
20-30 min Cooking time

ONE-POT CIDERED CHICKEN

ingredients	Metric	Imperial	American
Chicken portions	4	4	4
Flour	25 g	1 oz	1/4 cup
Butter	50 g	2 oz	1/4 cup
Onion, sliced	1	1	1
Dry cider	300 ml	1/2 pt	1 1/4 cups
Can button mushrooms	200 g	7 oz	7 oz
Can new potatoes	575 g	1 1/4 lb	1 1/4 lb
Can carrots	425 g	15 oz	15 oz
Can sweetcorn	350 g	12 oz	12 oz
Salt and pepper			
Garnish:			
Chopped fresh parsley			

method

1. Coat the chicken with the flour. Melt the butter in a pan and gently fry the onion and chicken until golden brown.

2. Add the cider, bring to the boil, cover and simmer over a low heat for 25-30 minutes.

3. Drain the mushrooms, potatoes, carrots and sweetcorn and add to the pan. Season.

4. Cook for a further 10-15 minutes until heated through. Serve garnished with chopped parsley.

5 min Preparation time
55 min Cooking time

PAPRIKA PORK

ingredients	Metric	Imperial	American
Lean diced pork	450 g	1 lb	1 lb
Flour	25 g	1 oz	1/4 cup
Butter	50 g	2 oz	1/4 cup
Large onion, diced	1	1	1
Paprika pepper	3 tsp	3 tsp	3 tsp
Can tomatoes	425 g	15 oz	15 oz
Chicken stock	300 ml	1/2 pt	1 1/4 cups
Salt and pepper			
Sour cream	150 ml	1/4 pt	2/3 cup
Garnish:			
Chopped fresh parsley			

method

1. Coat the pork in the flour. Melt the butter in a pan and fry the onion and pork until browned.

2. Add the paprika and cook for 1 minute. Add the tomatoes, stock and seasoning.

3. Cover and simmer for 40-45 minutes until the pork is tender, stirring occasionally. Alternatively, cook in the oven at 190°C/375°F/Gas Mark 5 for 1-1¼ hours.

4. Swirl in the cream and sprinkle with parsley before serving. Serve with rice or noodles.

variation

Use chicken breast instead of pork.

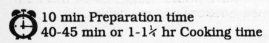
10 min Preparation time
40-45 min or 1-1¼ hr Cooking time

PORK FILLET IN SHERRY AND MUSHROOM SAUCE

ingredients	Metric	Imperial	American
Butter	*25 g*	*1 oz*	*2 tbsp*
Pork fillet (tenderloin), cut into 1cm/½ inch medallions	*675 g*	*1½ lb*	*1½ lb*
Large onion, sliced	*1*	*1*	*1*
Flour	*2 tbsp*	*2 tbsp*	*2 tbsp*
Paprika pepper	*1 tbsp*	*1 tbsp*	*1 tbsp*
Meat stock	*300 ml*	*½ pt*	*1¼ cups*
Salt and pepper			
Dry sherry	*4 tbsp*	*4 tbsp*	*4 tbsp*
Soured cream	*150 ml*	*¼ pt*	*⅔ cup*
Can sliced mushrooms, drained	*200 g*	*7 oz*	*7 oz*

method

1. Melt the butter in a pan and sauté the slices of pork fillet until browned. Remove from the pan.

2. Add the onion and fry until soft. Stir in the flour, paprika and gradually add the stock, stirring well to make a sauce.

3. Return the pork to the pan and coat with the sauce. Season, cover and simmer for 20 minutes until tender.

4. Add the sherry, soured cream and mushrooms. Heat through until simmering, but do not boil. Serve with new potatoes and vegetables.

variation

Spare rib or loin chops can also be used.

🕐 10 min Preparation time
40 min Cooking time

PORK WITH MUSTARD SAUCE

ingredients	Metric	Imperial	American
Butter	50 g	2 oz	¼ cup
Pork steak, cut into 1cm/ ½ inch strips	450 g	1 lb	1 lb
Flour	50 g	2 oz	½ cup
Milk	600 ml	1 pt	2 ½ cups
Whole grain mustard	2 tbsp	2 tbsp	2 tbsp
Squeeze of lemon juice			
Salt and pepper			
Garnish:			
Chopped fresh parsley			

method

1. Melt the butter in a pan and gently fry the pork strips until browned.

2. Stir in the flour and gradually add the milk, stirring continuously until the sauce thickens.

3. Add the remaining ingredients, cover and simmer for 10-15 minutes, stirring occasionally, until the pork is tender.

4. Serve on a bed of rice or noodles and garnish with parsley. Accompany with sweetcorn or French beans.

5 min Preparation time
25 min Cooking time

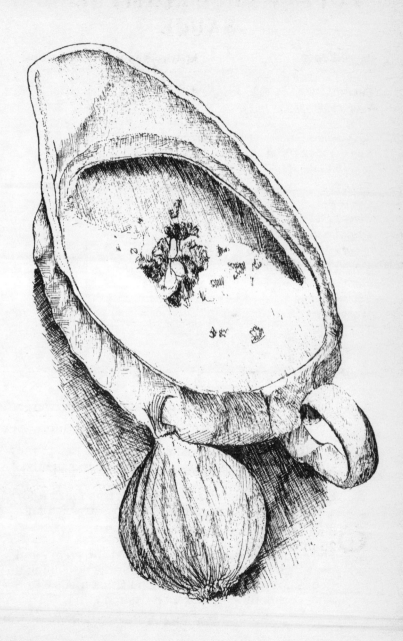

POUSSINS IN CREAMY WINE SAUCE

ingredients	Metric	Imperial	American
Poussins (rock Cornish game hens)	4	4	4
Flour	2 tbsp	2 tbsp	2 tbsp
White wine	150 ml	¼ pt	⅔ cup
Chicken stock (bouillon) cube, crumbled	1	1	1
Olive oil	2 tbsp	2 tbsp	2 tbsp
Garlic salt	1 tsp	1 tsp	1 tsp
Black pepper			
Grated rind and juice of 1 lemon			
Double (heavy) cream	150 ml	¼ pt	⅔ cup
Garnish:			
Lemon wedges			
Watercress			

method

1. Coat the poussins in the flour and place in a large casserole or prepared chicken brick.

2. Mix the remaining ingredients together, except the cream, and pour over the poussins. Cover tightly.

3. Bake in the oven at 200°C/400°F/Gas Mark 6 for 1-1 ¼ hours. Remove the poussins, arrange on a serving plate and keep warm.

4. Place the sauce in a saucepan, add the cream and heat through. Do not boil. Adjust the seasoning if necessary. (The sauce may be thickened with a little cornflour (cornstarch) if desired.)

5. Pour over the poussins and serve garnished with lemon wedges and watercress.

variation

This recipe is also suitable for chicken or turkey fillets.

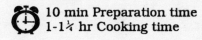 10 min Preparation time
1-1¼ hr Cooking time

RUMP STEAK STILTON

ingredients	Metric	Imperial	American
Butter	15 g	½ oz	1 tbsp
Rump steak, cut into 1cm/ ½ inch strips	450 g	1 lb	1 lb
Flour	15 g	½ oz	2 tbsp
Milk	150 ml	¼ pt	⅔ cup
White Stilton cheese, grated	50 g	2 oz	½ cup
Single (light) cream	150 ml	¼ pt	⅔ cup
Salt and pepper			

method

1. Melt the butter in a pan, add the steak and toss to seal for about 5 minutes. Stir in the flour and cook for 2 minutes.

2. Gradually add the milk, stirring until the sauce thickens and is smooth. Cook for 1 minute.

3. Add the Stilton and cream, season. Do not boil. Serve with sauté potatoes and broccoli.

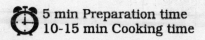 5 min Preparation time
10-15 min Cooking time

SAUSAGE CHILLI PIE

ingredients	Metric	Imperial	American
Continental sausage	450 g	1 lb	1 lb
Can kidney beans in chilli sauce	425 g	15 oz	15 oz
Instant or fresh mashed potato	675 g	1½ lb	3 cups

method

1. Slice the sausage, mix with the beans and heat until hot.

2. Place in a pie dish and pipe or fork over the mashed potato.

3. Place under a grill (broiler) until golden brown. Serve with salad and crusty bread.

variation

The kidney beans may be substituted for barbecue beans or baked beans.

 10 min Preparation time
10-15 min Cooking time

SAUSAGE GOULASH

ingredients	Metric	Imperial	American
Butter	25 g	1 oz	2 tbsp
Pork or beef sausages	450 g	1 lb	1 lb
Medium onion, chopped	1	1	1
Flour	1 tbsp	1 tbsp	1 tbsp
Carrots, peeled and sliced	225 g	8 oz	2 cups
Can chopped tomatoes	425 g	15 oz	15 oz

ingredients	Metric	Imperial	American
Can condensed tomato soup	425 g	15 oz	15 oz
Tomato purée (paste)	1 tbsp	1 tbsp	1 tbsp
Paprika pepper	1 tbsp	1 tbsp	1 tbsp
Potatoes, cut into 2.5cm/ 1 inch dice	450 g	1 lb	1 lb
Stock	300 ml	½ pt	1 ¼ cups
Salt and pepper			
Garnish:			
Sour cream			
Chopped fresh parsley			

method

1. Melt the butter in a pan and fry the sausages lightly. Transfer to a casserole.

2. Add the onion and sauté for 2 minutes. Stir in the flour and cook for a further minute.

3. Stir in the carrots, tomatoes, soup, tomato purée, paprika, potatoes and stock.

4. Adjust seasoning. Reheat until just boiling and pour over the sausages. Mix well.

5. Place a lid on the casserole and cook in the oven at 200°C/400°F/Gas Mark 6 for 50-60 minutes.

6. Remove lid, swirl in the sour cream, sprinkle with the parsley and serve with a green vegetable or warm crusty bread.

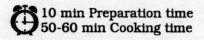 10 min Preparation time
50-60 min Cooking time

SAUTEED LIVER IN CREAM SAUCE

ingredients	Metric	Imperial	American
Butter	25 g	1 oz	2 tbsp
Large onion, chopped	1	1	1
Chicken livers, cut into strips	450 g	1 lb	1 lb
Single (light) cream	150 ml	¼ pt	⅔ cup
Milk	150 ml	¼ pt	⅔ cup
Salt and pepper			
Garnish:			
Paprika pepper			

method

1. Melt the butter in a pan and sauté the onion for 2 minutes. Add the livers and fry for 5 minutes, tossing well.

2. Stir in the cream, milk and seasoning. Simmer gently for 2 minutes, stirring occasionally.

3. Garnish with a sprinkling of paprika and serve with rice and a crisp green salad.

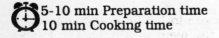 5-10 min Preparation time
10 min Cooking time

SAVOURY HASH FLAN

ingredients	Metric	Imperial	American
Baked shortcrust pastry flan case (basic pie dough shell)	18 cm	7 inch	7 inch
Butter	25 g	1 oz	2 tbsp
Medium onion, chopped	1	1	1
Green pepper, chopped	1	1	1
Potatoes, peeled and diced	175 g	6 oz	1½ cups
Milk	175 ml	6 fl oz	¾ cup
Can corned beef, diced	200 g	7 oz	7 oz
Chopped fresh parsley	1 tbsp	1 tbsp	1 tbsp
Salt and pepper			

method

1. Place the baked pastry case on a flat baking tray. Melt the butter in a pan and sauté the onion, pepper and potatoes for about 5 minutes until lightly browned.

2. Add the milk and simmer for a further 10 minutes. Add the beef, parsley and seasoning and cook until the liquid is absorbed.

3. Place the beef mixture in the flan case, spreading evenly. Bake in the oven at 190°C/375°F/Gas Mark 5 for 10-15 minutes until golden brown. Serve hot with vegetables or cold with salad.

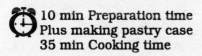
10 min Preparation time
Plus making pastry case
35 min Cooking time

SAVOURY MEAT LOAF

ingredients	Metric	Imperial	American
Streaky bacon rashers (slices), rinded	225 g	8 oz	8 oz
Cooked meat, minced (ground), see Note	225 g	8 oz	1 cup
Packet bread sauce mix	300 ml	½ pt	1 ¼ cups
Stuffing mix or breadcrumbs	25g	1 oz	⅓ cup
Medium onion, finely chopped	1	1	1
Tomato purée (paste) or ketchup	1 tbsp	1 tbsp	1 tbsp
Egg, beaten	1	1	1
Milk	150 ml	¼ pt	⅔ cup
Salt and pepper			

method

1. Grease a 450g/1 lb loaf tin (pan) and line with the rashers of bacon.

2. Mix together the meat, bread sauce mix, stuffing mix, onion, tomato purée, egg and milk.

3. Place in the loaf tin and cover with foil. Bake in the oven at 200°C/400°F/Gas Mark 6 for 1-1 ¼ hours.

4. Turn out and serve hot with vegetables and potatoes. Alternatively, cool in the tin and serve cold with salad.

note

Use the remainder of a joint, such as lamb, pork, beef, chicken.

10 min Preparation time
1-1¼ hr Cooking time

SOMERSET GAMMON ROAST

ingredients	Metric	Imperial	American
Gammon (smoked ham) joint, soaked	1 kg	2 ¼ lb	2 ¼ lb
Cider	300 ml	½ pt	1 ¼ cups
Sage	2 tsp	2 tsp	2 tsp
Apples, peeled and quartered	2	2	2
Lemon juice	2 tsp	2 tsp	2 tsp
Salt and pepper			
Little cornflour (cornstarch), optional			

method

1. Boil the gammon in a pan of water for 20 minutes.

2. Transfer to a casserole, pour over the cider and sprinkle with sage.

3. Cover and cook in the oven at 180°C/350°F/Gas Mark 4 for a further 30 minutes.

4. Toss the apples in the lemon juice, add to the gammon and cook uncovered for a further 30 minutes. Remove the gammon. Season, then thicken the sauce with a little cornflour, if wished. Serve with boiled potatoes and vegetables.

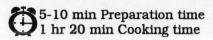 5-10 min Preparation time
1 hr 20 min Cooking time

SPICY SAUSAGE CASSEROLE

ingredients	Metric	Imperial	American
Butter	25 g	1 oz	2 tbsp
Large onion, chopped	1	1	1
Rinded streaky bacon rashers (slices), chopped	125 g	4 oz	½ cup
Frankfurters, garlic sausage or continental sausage, chopped	450 g	1 lb	1 lb
Flour	25 g	1 oz	¼ cup
Can red kidney beans, drained	425 g	15 oz	15 oz
Can chopped tomatoes	425 g	15 oz	15 oz
Stock	300 ml	½ pt	1 ¼ cups
Tomato purée (paste)	2 tbsp	2 tbsp	2 tbsp
Brown sauce	1 tbsp	1 tbsp	1 tbsp
Salt and pepper			

method

1. Melt the butter in a pan and sauté the onion and bacon until lightly browned.

2. Add all the remaining ingredients and cook for 10 minutes. Serve with rice or noodles and vegetables.

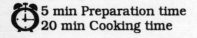 5 min Preparation time
20 min Cooking time

SWEET AND SOUR SPARE RIBS

ingredients	Metric	Imperial	American
Spare (country-style) ribs, cut	1.8 kg	4 lb	4 lb
Salt			
Oil	2 tbsp	2 tbsp	2 tbsp
Sauce:			
Tomato purée	1 tbsp	1 tbsp	1 tbsp
Soy sauce	3 tbsp	3 tbsp	3 tbsp
Worcestershire sauce	1 tbsp	1 tbsp	1 tbsp
Soft brown sugar	1 tbsp	1 tbsp	1 tbsp
Clear honey	1 tbsp	1 tbsp	1 tbsp
Ginger	½ tsp	½ tsp	½ tsp
Lemon juice	1 tbsp	1 tbsp	1 tbsp
Chicken stock	300 ml	½ pt	1 ¼ cups
Black pepper			
Garnish:			
Orange, segmented	1	1	1

method

1. Place the ribs in a roasting tin (pan), sprinkle with salt and oil. Bake in the oven at 190°C/375°F/ Gas Mark 5 for 30 minutes.

2. Combine the sauce ingredients and pour over the ribs, tossing well to coat them. Cover with foil and bake for a further 1 - 1 ½ hours, turning in the sauce frequently during cooking. Remove the foil 30 minutes before the end of the cooking time to thicken the sauce.

3. Serve on a platter, garnished with orange segments with a bowl of boiled rice.

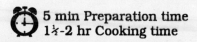 5 min Preparation time
1½-2 hr Cooking time

TIPSY CHEESE CHOPS

ingredients	Metric	Imperial	American
Double loin lamb chops, 175g/6 oz each	4	4	4
Can chopped mushrooms, drained	200 g	7 oz	7 oz
Glass of white wine	1	1	1
Cheddar cheese, grated	100 g	4 oz	1 cup
Salt and pepper			

method

1. Cook the chops under a medium grill (broiler) for 7-8 minutes on each side.

2. Place the remaining ingredients in a saucepan and heat gently until the cheese has melted and the sauce is smooth.

3. Place a spoonful on top of each chop and grill until browned.

4. Serve with any remaining sauce, potatoes and a green vegetable.

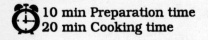 10 min Preparation time
20 min Cooking time

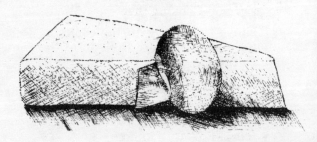

TURKEY MINCE BURGERS

ingredients	Metric	Imperial	American
Turkey mince	450 g	1 lb	2 cups
Medium onion, chopped	1	1	1
Garlic purée	2 tsp	2 tsp	2 tsp
Chopped fresh parsley	1 tsp	1 tsp	1 tsp
Worcestershire sauce	2 tsp	2 tsp	2 tsp
Salt and pepper			
Baps	4	4	4
Jar red wine and herb sauce	265 g	9 oz	9 oz

method

1. Place the turkey mince, onion, garlic purée, parsley, Worcestershire sauce and seasoning in a bowl. Mix well and shape into 4 burgers.

2. Place under a hot grill (broiler) and seal on both sides. Reduce the heat and cook for 10-15 minutes, turning over halfway through cooking time.

3. Heat the jar of sauce, place the burgers in the baps and spoon the sauce on top. Serve with salad or coleslaw and French fries.

🕐 10 min Preparation time
20 min Cooking time

VEGETARIAN BOLOGNESE

ingredients	Metric	Imperial	American
Butter	50 g	2 oz	¼ cup
Large onion, chopped	1	1	1
Cloves of garlic or 2 tsp garlic purée	2	2	2
200g/7 oz cans sliced mushrooms, drained	2	2	2
Walnut halves	100 g	4 oz	1 cup
Can chopped tomatoes	200 g	7 oz	7 oz
Can tomato purée (paste)	75 g	3 oz	3 oz
Mixed herbs	½ tsp	½ tsp	½ tsp
Black (ripe) olives (reserve a few for garnish)			
Salt and pepper			
Spaghetti	450 g	1 lb	1 lb
Garnish:			
Chopped fresh parsley			

method

1. Melt the butter in a pan and sauté the onion and garlic until browned.

2. Add the mushrooms, walnuts, tomatoes, tomato purée, herbs and olives. Cover and simmer for 10-15 minutes. Season.

3. While the sauce is simmering, cook the spaghetti in salted water for 10-15 minutes.

4. Drain, place on a serving dish with the sauce poured over the top. Garnish with the remaining olives and chopped parsley.

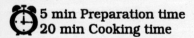 5 min Preparation time
20 min Cooking time

VEGETABLE CURRY

ingredients	Metric	Imperial	American
Butter	25 g	1 oz	2 tbsp
Large onion, chopped	1	1	1
Curry powder, or to taste	1 tbsp	1 tbsp	1 tbsp
Tomato purée (paste)	1 tbsp	1 tbsp	1 tbsp
Chutney or sweet pickle	1 tbsp	1 tbsp	1 tbsp
Lemon juice	1 tsp	1 tsp	1 tsp
Raisins or sultanas (golden raisins), optional	50 g	2 oz	1/3 cup
425g/15 oz cans cream of vegetable soup	2	2	2
Mixed vegetables, fresh or frozen, cooked	1 kg	2 lb	2 lb
Garnish:			
Hard-boiled (hard cooked) eggs	4	4	4

method

1. Melt the butter in a pan and sauté the onion for 2-3 minutes until tender. Add the curry powder and cook for a further 2 minutes.

2. Stir in the tomato purée, chutney, lemon juice, raisins and soup. Cover and simmer for 10 minutes.

3. Add the vegetables, stir into the curry sauce and heat through.

4. Serve garnished with sliced or quartered hard-boiled eggs and boiled rice. Chutney and diced cucumber in natural yoghurt are excellent accompaniments to this dish.

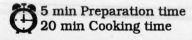 5 min Preparation time
20 min Cooking time

VEGETABLE HOT POT

ingredients	Metric	Imperial	American
Butter	50 g	2 oz	1/4 cup
Mixed vegetables, cut into bite sized pieces	900 g	2 lb	2 lb
425g/15 oz cans cream of vegetable soup	2	2	2
Vegetable stock	300 ml	1/2 pt	1 1/4 cups
Potatoes, peeled and thinly sliced	450 g	1 lb	1 lb
Salt and pepper			
Knobs of butter	6	6	6

method

1. Melt the butter in a large pan and add the mixed vegetables. Fry for a few minutes, tossing well until browned.

2. Add the soup and stock. Bring to the boil, then remove from the heat.

3. Lay half of the potatoes in the base of a casserole. Pour the vegetable mix on top and finish with another layer of potatoes. Season and dot with knobs of butter.

4. Cover and bake in the oven at 200°C/400°F/Gas Mark 6 for about 1-1 ¼ hours. Remove the lid 20 minutes before the end of the cooking time to brown the potatoes.

note

Use vegetables in season, such as leek, cauliflower, celery, swede, onions, carrots, etc. or large cut frozen vegetables.

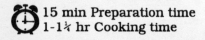 15 min Preparation time
1-1 ¼ hr Cooking time

VIKING LAMB CUTLETS

ingredients	Metric	Imperial	American
Best end lamb cutlets (rib chops)	8	8	8
Packet onion sauce mix	300 ml	½ pt	1 ¼ cup
Capers, chopped	1 tbsp	1 tbsp	1 tbsp
Gherkins (dill pickles), sliced	4	4	4
Salt and pepper			
Garnish:			
Stuffed olives, sliced	6	6	6

method

1. Grill (broil) the lamb cutlets over medium heat.

2. While cooking, make up the onion sauce mix according to directions. Add the capers and gherkins and adjust seasoning if necessary.

3. Serve the cutlets coated with the viking sauce. Garnish with sliced olives. Serve with new potatoes and buttered sweetcorn.

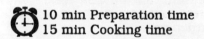 10 min Preparation time
15 min Cooking time

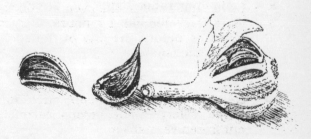

WHOLESOME TURKEY CASSEROLE

ingredients	Metric	Imperial	American
Butter	25 g	1 oz	2 tbsp
Turkey meat, diced	450 g	1 lb	1 lb
Baby onions, frozen	225 g	8 oz	8 oz
Baby sweetcorn, frozen	225 g	8 oz	1 ½ cups
Can condensed mushroom soup	425 g	15 oz	15 oz
Salt and pepper			
Garnish:			
Chopped fresh parsley			

method

1. Melt the butter in a pan and fry the turkey until lightly browned.

2. Add the onions, sweetcorn and soup. Bring to the boil, cover and simmer for 45 minutes until the meat is tender. Season.

3. Serve on a bed of rice and garnish with parsley. Accompany with garden peas.

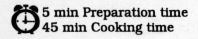 5 min Preparation time
45 min Cooking time

SALAds ANd Cold MEAls

CELERY ROULADE

ingredients	Metric	Imperial	American
Can celery hearts	524 g	1lb 2 ½ oz	1lb 2 ½ oz
Slices ham	4	4	4
Lettuce leaves			
Lemon juice	1 tsp	1 tsp	1 tsp
Mayonnaise	4 tbsp	4 tbsp	4 tbsp
Garnish:			
Lemon wedges	4	4	4

method

1. Drain the celery hearts and divide into 4 portions.

2. Wrap a slice of ham around each one and arrange on a bed of lettuce.

3. Combine the lemon juice and mayonnaise and spoon over the centre of each roll.

4. Garnish with lemon. Serve with salad.

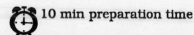 10 min preparation time

CHEESE 'N' NUTTY EGGS

ingredients	Metric	Imperial	American
Hard-boiled (hard cooked) eggs, shelled	4	4	4
Cottage cheese and chives	25 g	1 oz	2 tbsp
Cheddar cheese, grated	25 g	1 oz	¼ cup
Single (light) cream	3 tbsp	3 tbsp	3 tbsp
Salted peanuts, chopped	25 g	1 oz	¼ cup
Salt and pepper			
Garnish:			
Paprika pepper			
Shredded lettuce			

method

1. Cut the eggs in half lengthways. Remove the yolks and place in a bowl.

2. Add the cheeses, cream, nuts and seasoning. Mix well.

3. Spoon or pipe into the egg cases and sprinkle with paprika. Serve on a bed of shredded lettuce. Use as a starter or an accompaniment to a salad.

variation

Use cottage cheese and pineapple instead of cottage cheese and chives.

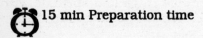 15 min Preparation time

108

COTTAGE CHEESE AND SHRIMP SALAD

ingredients	Metric	Imperial	American
Cottage cheese or cottage cheese and chives	225 g	8 oz	1 cup
Single (light) cream or mayonnaise	3 tbsp	3 tbsp	3 tbsp
Prawns or shrimps, fresh, frozen or canned (drained)	225 g	8 oz	1⅓ cups
Celery sticks, sliced	4	4	4
Small red or green pepper (or mixed,) chopped	1	1	1
Salt and pepper			
Garnish:			
Crisp green lettuce			
Can pineapple rings, drained	225 g	8 oz	8 oz
Paprika pepper			

method

1. Combine the cottage cheese, cream, prawns or shrimps, celery, pepper and seasoning.

2. Arrange the lettuce on a platter and place the salad mixture in the centre.

3. Garnish with pineapple rings and sprinkle with paprika. Serve with French or granary bread and a side salad.

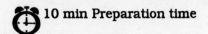 10 min Preparation time

HARLEQUIN PASTA SALAD

ingredients	Metric	Imperial	American
Mayonnaise	6 tbsp	6 tbsp	6 tbsp
Pasta shapes or shells, cooked	350 g	12 oz	3 cups
Can sweetcorn (corn kernels), drained	350 g	12 oz	12 oz
Can pimentos, chopped (reserve 1 tbsp for garnish)	175 g	6 oz	6 oz
Ham (cooked), chopped	225 g	8 oz	1 cup
Stuffed olives, halved (reserve a few for garnish)	12	12	12
Salt and pepper			

method

1. Thin the mayonnaise slightly with a little water.

2. Place all the ingredients in a bowl, season and toss well to coat with dressing.

3. Place in a salad bowl and garnish with reserved pimento and olives. Serve chilled.

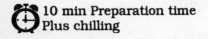 10 min Preparation time
Plus chilling

HARLEQUIN PEPPER SALAD

ingredients	Metric	Imperial	American
Tomatoes, sliced	450 g	1 lb	1 lb
Red pepper, sliced	1	1	1
Green pepper, sliced	1	1	1
Yellow pepper, sliced	1	1	1
Large onion, sliced	1	1	1
Dressing:			
Wine vinegar	2 tbsp	2 tbsp	2 tbsp
Olive oil	4 tbsp	4 tbsp	4 tbsp
Mustard or to taste	1 tsp	1 tsp	1 tsp
Caster (superfine) sugar	½ tsp	½ tsp	½ tsp
Salt and pepper			

method

1. Layer the tomatoes, peppers and onion in a salad bowl.

2. Place all the ingredients for the dressing in a glass jar and shake well until mixed.

3. Pour the dressing over the salad, then chill well before serving.

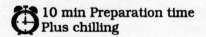 10 min Preparation time
Plus chilling

MUSHROOM SALAD

ingredients	Metric	Imperial	American
Button mushrooms	225 g	8 oz	2 cups
Dressing:			
Mayonnaise	3 tbsp	3 tbsp	3 tbsp
Cream or natural yoghurt	3 tbsp	3 tbsp	3 tbsp
Creamed horseradish	1 tbsp	1 tbsp	1 tbsp
Lemon juice	1 tsp	1 tsp	1 tsp
Salt and pepper			
Garnish:			
Chopped fresh parsley			

method

1. Wash the mushrooms and pat dry. Quarter them.

2. Place the dressing ingredients in a bowl and mix well.

3. Add the mushrooms and stir until well coated with dressing.

4. Place in a serving bowl, sprinkle with parsley and chill before serving.

10 min Preparation time
Plus chilling

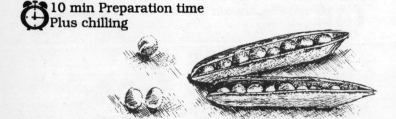

NAPOLINA SALAD

ingredients	Metric	Imperial	American
Iceberg lettuce, shredded	½	½	½
Bunch spring onions (scallions), chopped	1	1	1
Tomatoes, quartered	450 g	1 lb	1 lb
Black (ripe) olives	50 g	2 oz	⅓ cup
Mozzarella cheese, cubed	100 g	4 oz	1 cup
Cloves garlic, crushed	2	2	2
Salt and pepper			
Salad dressing	4 tbsp	4 tbsp	4 tbsp

method

1. Place all the salad ingredients, except the dressing, in a bowl and toss well. Chill.

2. Sprinkle with salad dressing just before serving. Serve with kebabs or pitta bread.

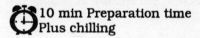
10 min Preparation time
Plus chilling

POTATO AND SPRING ONION SALAD

ingredients	Metric	Imperial	American
Potatoes, boiled fresh or canned , drained and diced	750 g	1½ lb	1½ lb
Bunch spring onions (scallions), chopped	1	1	1
Bacon, crisply fried and crumbled	50 g	2 oz	½ cup
Mayonnaise	4 tbsp	4 tbsp	4 tbsp
Lemon juice	1 tbsp	1 tbsp	1 tbsp
Salt and pepper			
Garnish:			
Sesame or poppy seeds	1 tbsp	1 tbsp	1 tbsp

method

1. Place all the ingredients, except the garnish, in a bowl. Toss until well mixed.

2. Serve chilled, sprinkled with sesame or poppy seeds.

🕐 10-15 min Preparation time
Plus chilling

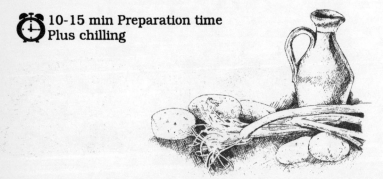

STIR-FRY SALAD

ingredients	Metric	Imperial	American
Can pineapple pieces	200 g	7 oz	7 oz
Packet stir-fry vegetables, cooked	450 g	1 lb	1 lb
Brown rice, cooked	100 g	4 oz	¾ cup
Soy sauce	2 tbsp	2 tbsp	2 tbsp
Worcestershire sauce	1 tbsp	1 tbsp	1 tbsp
Pineapple syrup	2 tbsp	2 tbsp	2 tbsp
Salt and pepper			

method

1. Drain the pineapple pieces, reserving the syrup.

2. Place all the ingredients in a bowl. Toss well until coated in the dressing.

3. Chill and serve with cold meat or use to fill pitta breads.

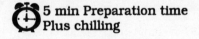 5 min Preparation time
Plus chilling

SWEETCORN COLESLAW

ingredients	Metric	Imperial	American
Small white cabbage	½	½	½
Can sweetcorn and peppers, drained	350 g	12 oz	12 oz
Can sliced mushrooms, drained	200 g	7 oz	7 oz
Mayonnaise	4-5 tbsp	4-5 tbsp	4-5 tbsp
Salt and pepper			
Garnish:			
Chopped fresh parsley			

method

1. Finely shred the cabbage and place in a bowl.

2. Add all the remaining ingredients and toss well. Chill. Serve sprinkled with chopped parsley.

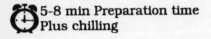 5-8 min Preparation time
Plus chilling

THREE BEAN SALAD

ingredients	Metric	Imperial	American
Can red kidney beans	425 g	15 oz	15 oz
Can chick (garbanzo) peas	425 g	15 oz	15 oz
Can haricot (navy) beans	425 g	15 oz	15 oz
Small onion, sliced, or spring onions (scallions) or chives, chopped	1	1	1
French dressing	6 tbsp	6 tbsp	6 tbsp

method

1. Drain the cans of beans and peas, then place in a bowl.

2. Add the onion. Toss the salad with the French dressing. Serve chilled.

5 min Preparation time
Plus chilling

WALDORF CHICKEN SALAD

ingredients	Metric	Imperial	American
Cooked chicken, diced	450 g	1 lb	1 lb
Cooked rice	125 g	4 oz	1 cup
Red eating apples, diced	2	2	2
Sticks celery, sliced	4	4	4
Sultanas (golden raisins) or raisins	25 g	1 oz	3 tbsp
Walnut pieces	25 g	1 oz	¼ cup
Mayonnaise	6 tbsp	6 tbsp	6 tbsp
Water	1 tbsp	1 tbsp	1 tbsp
Salt and pepper			
Garnish:			
Apple slices			
Lemon juice			
Chopped fresh parsley			

method

1. Place the chicken, rice, apple (reserve a few slices for garnish), celery, sultanas and walnuts in a bowl. Stir to combine.

2. Mix the mayonnaise and water, then pour over the chicken mixture. Season and fold in until well coated with dressing.

3. Place the salad in a large salad bowl and garnish with apple slices, dipped in a little lemon juice, and parsley. Serve chilled with a green salad and tomatoes.

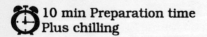 10 min Preparation time
Plus chilling

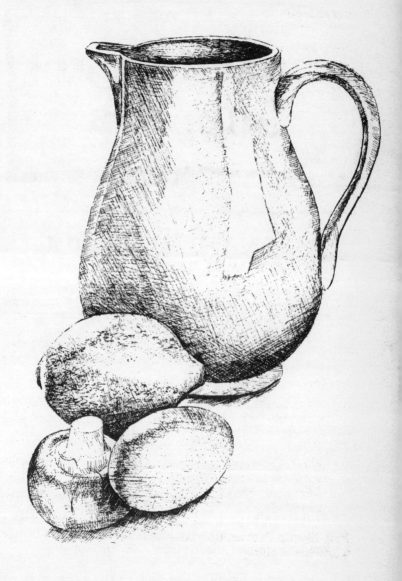

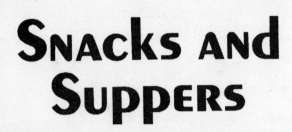

Snacks and Suppers

BACON AND MUSHROOM COBS

ingredients	Metric	Imperial	American
Round crusty rolls	4	4	4
Butter	50 g	2 oz	¼ cup
Packet white sauce mix	300 ml	½ pt	1¼ cups
Can sliced mushrooms, drained	175 g	6 oz	6 oz
Cooked bacon or ham, diced	100 g	4 oz	½ cup
Salt and pepper			
Chopped fresh parsley	1 tbsp	1 tbsp	1 tbsp

method

1. Slice the tops from the rolls and scoop out the centres (use to make breadcrumbs). Melt the butter and brush the inside of the rolls and tops.

2. Place on a baking tray and bake in the oven at 200°C/400°F/ Gas Mark 6 for about 5 minutes until golden.

3. While baking the rolls, make up the sauce mix according to directions. Add the mushrooms, bacon, seasoning and parsley.

4. Fill the rolls with the mixture, replace the tops and serve with a crisp salad.

variation

Use diced chicken instead of bacon.

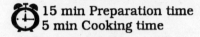 15 min Preparation time
5 min Cooking time

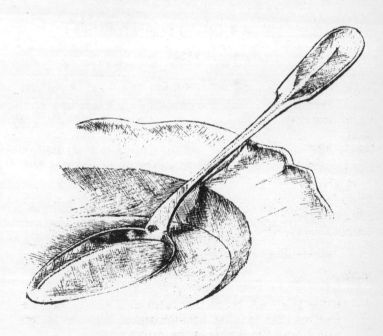

CAULIFLOWER GRATINE

ingredients	Metric	Imperial	American
Medium cauliflower or 350g/12 oz frozen	1	1	1
Packet white sauce mix	300 ml	½ pt	1¼ cup
Bacon or ham, cooked and chopped	100 g	4 oz	½ cup
Can sliced mushrooms, drained	200 g	7 oz	7 oz
Salt and pepper			
Dried breadcrumbs or 1 packet crisps, crushed	2 tbsp	2 tbsp	2 tbsp
Garnish:			
Chopped fresh parsley			

method

1. Prepare and cook the cauliflower. Place in a shallow dish.

2. Make up the sauce mix according to instructions. Add the bacon and mushrooms. Adjust the seasoning.

3. Pour the sauce over the cauliflower, sprinkle with the breadcrumbs and brown under a hot grill (broiler) or in the oven. Serve garnished with a sprinkling of parsley.

10 min Preparation time
25 min Cooking time

CHEESY SAUSAGE PUFF ROLL

ingredients	Metric	Imperial	American
Frozen puff pastry, thawed	225 g	8 oz	8 oz
Beef sausagemeat	450 g	1 lb	2 cups
Tomato ketchup	4 tbsp	4 tbsp	4 tbsp
Cheddar cheese, grated	100 g	4 oz	1 cup
Beaten egg to glaze			

method

1. Roll out the pastry to an oblong 25 x 30 cm/10 x 12 inches.

2. Spread the sausagemeat over the pastry to within 2.5 cm/1 inch of the edges. Spread with the ketchup and sprinkle with cheese.

3. Brush the edges with egg and roll up loosely from the long side. Seal the ends by pinching together or pressing with a fork. Make a pattern on the top with the back of a knife.

4. Place on a baking sheet and brush with egg. Bake in the oven at 220°C/425°F/Gas Mark 7 for 35-40 minutes until risen and golden brown. Serve hot with potatoes and vegetables or cold with salad.

variation

Substitute the tomato ketchup with brown sauce or 2 teaspoons mustard.

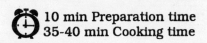 10 min Preparation time
35-40 min Cooking time

CHEESE AND VEGETABLE SCRAMBLE

ingredients	Metric	Imperial	American
Potatoes, peeled and sliced	450 g	1 lb	1 lb
Mixed vegetables, cut into large dice, such as cauliflower, carrots, green beans, peas, mushrooms	800 g	1¾ lb	1¾ lb
Cheddar or Cheshire cheese, grated	100 g	4 oz	1 cup
Eggs	4	4	4
Milk	600 ml	1 pt	2 ½ cups
Salt and pepper			

method

1. Layer the potatoes, vegetables and cheese in a casserole, finishing with a layer of cheese.

2. Beat the eggs and milk, season and pour over the vegetables.

3. Bake in the oven at 180°C/350°F/Gas Mark 4 for 1¼-1½ hours until set and golden brown. Serve with cold meat or baked fish.

note

Fresh or frozen vegetables may be used.

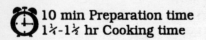 10 min Preparation time
1¼-1½ hr Cooking time

CRUNCHY VEGETABLE LAYER

ingredients	Metric	Imperial	American
Packet parsley sauce mix	300 ml	½ pt	1 ¼ cups
Cooked vegetables	750 g	1 ½ lb	1 ½ lb
Topping:			
Packet stuffing mix	50 g	2 oz	½ cup
Cheddar cheese, grated	50 g	2 oz	½ cup
Butter	25 g	1 oz	2 tbsp

method

1. Make up the sauce mix according to directions.

2. Add the vegetables and toss well until coated. Place in a casserole.

3. Mix the stuffing with the cheese and rub in the butter. Sprinkle over the vegetables.

4. Bake in the oven at 200°C/400°F/Gas Mark 6 for 30-40 minutes until the vegetables are hot and the topping golden and crisp. Serve with cold meat or French bread.

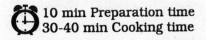

10 min Preparation time
30-40 min Cooking time

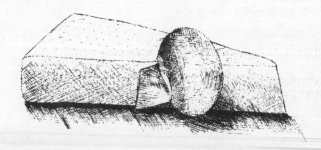

DEEP PAN OMELETTE

ingredients	Metric	Imperial	American
Eggs	8	8	8
Mixed herbs	½ tsp	½ tsp	½ tsp
Salt and pepper			
Butter	25 g	1 oz	2 tbsp
Leftover cooked vegetables, such as potatoes, carrots, onions, peas etc	225 g	8 oz	8 oz

method

1. Place the eggs in a bowl with the herbs and seasoning. Beat well until light and fluffy.

2. Melt the butter in a large frying pan (skillet) and toss the vegetables for 2-3 minutes.

3. Pour in the eggs and cook gently for 5-8 minutes until the underneath is set.

4. Place the pan under a hot grill (broiler) to set the omelette and lightly brown the surface. (If a grill is not available the omelette will set if allowed slightly longer to cook.) Serve with crisp green salad and crusty bread.

5 min Preparation time
10-15 min Cooking time

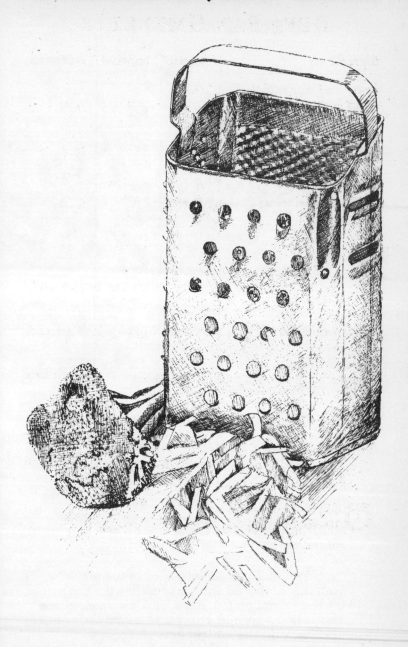

DEEP PAN PIZZA

ingredients	Metric	Imperial	American
Packet pizza base mix	150 g	5 oz	5 oz
Milk to mix			
Butter	25 g	1 oz	2 tbsp
Topping 1:			
450 g/1 lb jar of any pasta sauce	½	½	½
Salami, thinly sliced	100 g	4 oz	4 oz
Cheddar cheese, grated	50 g	2 oz	½ cup
Topping 2:			
Jar tomato spaghetti sauce	350 g	12 oz	12 oz
Can sliced mushrooms, drained	200 g	7 oz	7 oz
Cheddar cheese, grated	75 g	3 oz	¾ cup
Topping 3:			
Jar spaghetti bolognese sauce	450 g	1 lb	1 lb
Mozzarella cheese, sliced	100 g	4 oz	1 cup

method

1. Make up the pizza dough according to directions, using milk in place of water.

2. Knead well and roll out to a 20-23cm/8-9 inch round to fit the base of a frying pan (skillet).

3. Melt the butter and fry gently on one side until golden brown.

4. Turn over and spread with ONE of the toppings.
    Topping 1, spread the pizza base with the sauce, lay the salami on top and sprinkle with cheese.
    Topping 2, spread the pizza base with sauce, sprinkel with the mushrooms and cheese.
    Topping 3, spread the pizza base with the sauce and cover with the mozzarella.

5. Cover the frying pan while the underside of the pizza is cooking to heat the topping through. Flash under a hot grill (broiler) to brown the topping. Serve with salad.

 10-15 min Preparation time
10 min Cooking time

HAWAIIAN CRUMPETS

ingredients	Metric	Imperial	American
Crumpets, muffins or rounds of bread	4	4	4
Cheddar cheese, grated, or 4 cheese slices	100 g	4 oz	1 cup
Small round ham steaks	4	4	4
Canned pineapple rings, drained	4	4	4
Garnish:			
Pickle, glacé (candied) cherries or sliced tomato			

method

1. Lightly butter a flat baking tin.

2. Sprinkle each crumpet with the cheese, place a ham steak on top of this and top with a pineapple ring.

3. Place on the shelf above centre of the oven at 200°C/400°F/Gas Mark 6 for 10-12 minutes until the cheese has melted and ham is cooked.

4. Fill the centre of the pineapple with a spoonful of pickle, a glacé cherry or sliced tomato. Serve hot.

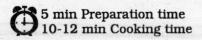 5 min Preparation time
10-12 min Cooking time

HOT TUNA AND RICE PITTA

ingredients	Metric	Imperial	American
Pitta breads	4	4	4
Filling:			
Can tuna	200 g	7 oz	7 oz
Long grain rice, cooked	175 g	6 oz	1 cup
Spring onions (scallions), chopped (chives may also be used)	6	6	6
Mayonnaise	6 tbsp	6 tbsp	6 tbsp
Lemon juice	2 tsp	2 tsp	2 tsp
Salt and pepper			

method

1. Cut the pittas in half and insert a knife through the centre of each to form pockets.

2. Place the filling ingredients in a bowl and mix well.

3. Spoon the filling into the pittas and place on an ovenproof dish. Heat in the oven at 200°C/400°F/Gas Mark 6 for 15-20 minutes until heated through.

variation

This filling may also be served cold or as a salad.

8-10 min Preparation time
15-20 min Cooking time

JAMBOREE PANCAKES

ingredients	Metric	Imperial	American
Packet pancake batter mix	300 ml	½ pt	1¼ cups
Butter	25 g	1 oz	2 tbsp
Medium onion, chopped	1	1	1
Can corned beef, chopped	350 g	12 oz	12oz
Can condensed tomato soup	425 g	15oz	15 oz
Packet crisps, crushed, or breadcrumbs	25 g	1oz	1oz

method

1. Make up the batter mix according to instructions. Cook 8 pancakes.

2. Melt the butter in a pan and sauté the onion until golden brown. Add the corned beef and fry, tossing well, for 2 minutes.

3. Divide the mixture between the pancakes, roll up and arrange in a dish.

4. Pour the soup over the centre and sprinkle with the crisps.

5. Bake in the oven at 190°C/375°F/Gas Mark 5 for 15-20 minutes until heated through.

variation

Use chopped ham and pork and condensed mushroom soup.

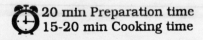
20 min Preparation time
15-20 min Cooking time

LYONNAISE POTATO CHEESE BAKE

ingredients	Metric	Imperial	American
Potatoes, peeled and thinly sliced	900 g	2 lb	2 lb
Large onion, thinly sliced	1	1	1
Butter, melted	50 g	2 oz	1/4 cup
Strong Cheddar cheese, grated	175 g	6 oz	1 1/2 cups
Salt and pepper			
Stock	300 ml	1/2 pt	1 1/4 cups
Garnish:			
Chopped fresh parsley			

method

1. Layer the potatoes, onion, butter and cheese in a casserole, seasoning each layer and finishing with cheese and butter.

2. Pour over the stock. Bake in the oven at 190°C/375°F/Gas Mark 5 for 1 1/4-1 1/2 hours until the potatoes are tender and the top is golden brown. Garnish with parsley before serving.

10 min Preparation time
1 1/4-1 1/2 hr Cooking time

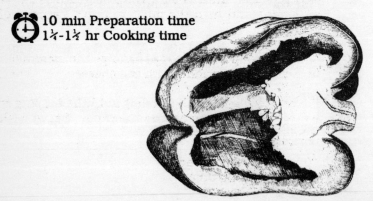

132

RICE CASSEROLE

ingredients	Metric	Imperial	American
Chicken stock	600 ml	1 pt	2 ½ cups
Brown rice	225 g	8 oz	1 ¼ cups
Medium onion, chopped	1	1	1
Ham, chopped	225 g	8 oz	1 cup
Can button mushrooms, drained	225 g	8 oz	8 oz
Can sweetcorn (corn kernels) and peppers, drained	350 g	12 oz	12 oz
Salt and pepper			
Topping:			
Can condensed mushroom soup	300 g	10 oz	10 oz
Can asparagus, drained	300 g	10 oz	10 oz
Cheddar cheese, grated	100 g	4 oz	1 cup

method

1. Bring the stock to the boil and add the rice and onion. Cover and simmer for 20 minutes, stirring occasionally.

2. Add the ham, mushrooms and sweetcorn. Adjust seasoning and turn the mixture into a flameproof casserole.

3. Pour the soup over the top, arrange the asparagus in a circle and sprinkle with the cheese.

4. Place under a hot grill (broiler) until the topping is heated and the cheese has melted. Serve with whole grilled tomatoes.

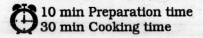 10 min Preparation time
30 min Cooking time

SAUSAGE BURGERS

ingredients	Metric	Imperial	American
Packet stuffing mix	25 g	1 oz	⅓ cup
Beef sausagemeat	450 g	1 lb	1 lb
Horseradish sauce	4 tsp	4 tsp	4 tsp
Baps	4	4	4

method

1. Make up the stuffing mix according to directions, then cool.

2. Combine all the ingredients, except the baps, and shape into 4 burgers.

3. Grill (broil) or fry for about 10 minutes, turning once. Serve in baps with onion rings and a side salad.

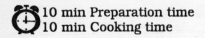 10 min Preparation time
10 min Cooking time

SAUSAGE SPIRAL ROLLS

ingredients	Metric	Imperial	American
Streaky bacon rashers (slices), rinded	8	8	8
Large pork sausages	8	8	8
Finger rolls	8	8	8
Relish, mustard or ketchup			

method

1. Wrap a rasher of bacon spirally around each sausage.

2. Cook in the oven at 200°C/400°F/Gas Mark 6 for about 30 minutes until browned.

3. Serve in the finger rolls with relish, mustard or ketchup.

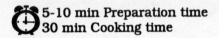 5-10 min Preparation time
30 min Cooking time

SPICED RICE

ingredients	Metric	Imperial	American
Butter	25 g	1 oz	2 tbsp
Large onion, chopped	1	1	1
Curry powder	1 tsp	1 tsp	1 tsp
Paprika pepper	1 tsp	1 tsp	1 tsp
Long grain rice	225 g	8 oz	1 ¼ cups
Meat stock	450 ml- 600 ml	¾ pt- 1 pt	2 cups- 2 ½ cups
Salt and pepper			

method

1. Melt the butter in a pan and sauté the onion until browned. Add the remaining ingredients. Stir well.

2. Cover and cook for 30 minutes, stirring occasionally, until the liquid has been absorbed and the rice is tender. Serve with grilled meat.

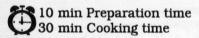
10 min Preparation time
30 min Cooking time

STUFFED PEPPERS WITH CHEESE SAUCE

ingredients	Metric	Imperial	American
Large red or green peppers	4	4	4
Butter	25 g	1 oz	2 tbsp
Medium onion, chopped	1	1	1
Bacon or ham, cooked and chopped	175 g	6 oz	¾ cup
Rice, cooked	175 g	6 oz	1 cup
Tomato ketchup	2 tbsp	2 tbsp	2 tbsp
Brown sauce or Worcestershire sauce	1 tbsp	1 tbsp	1 tbsp
Salt and pepper			
Packet cheese sauce mix	300 ml	½ pt	1¼ cups
Cheddar cheese, grated	25 g	1 oz	¼ cup

method

1. Cut the tops off the peppers, remove the seeds and blanch for 5 minutes in boiling water. Drain.

2. Melt the butter in a pan and sauté the onion for 2 minutes. Add the bacon, rice, ketchup, brown sauce and seasoning.

3. Fill the peppers with the rice mixture and place in an ovenproof dish.

4. Make up the sauce mix according to directions. Pour around the peppers and top each with grated cheese.

5. Bake in the oven at 180°C/350°F/Gas Mark 4 for 30-40 minutes until hot. Serve with salad and crusty bread.

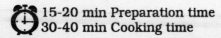 15-20 min Preparation time
30-40 min Cooking time

TUNA AND MUSHROOM PASTA

ingredients	Metric	Imperial	American
Pasta shapes, such as shells, bows etc.	225 g	8 oz	8 oz
Can condensed mushroom soup	300 g	10 oz	10 oz
Can tuna, flaked	200 g	7 oz	7 oz
Single (light) cream	150 ml	¼ pt	⅔ cup
Chopped fresh parsley	2 tsp	2 tsp	2 tsp
Salt and pepper			
Garnish:			
Can creamed or sliced mushrooms	175 g	6 oz	6 oz
Chopped fresh parsley			

method

1. Cook the pasta in a pan of salted water until tender.

2. While cooking, heat up the soup to simmering point. Add the tuna, cream and parsley. Season to taste. Heat through but do not boil.

3. Drain the pasta and toss gently with the sauce. Serve immediately garnished with warmed mushrooms and parsley.

🕐 10 min Preparation time
12-15 min Cooking time

VEGETABLE RISOTTO

ingredients	Metric	Imperial	American
Oil	2 tbsp	2 tbsp	2 tbsp
Large onion, sliced	1	1	1
Long grain rice	225 g	8 oz	1 ¼ cups
Chicken or vegetable stock	700 ml-825 ml	1 ¼ pts-1 ½ pts	3 cups-3 ¾ cups
Fresh or frozen vegetables, diced	450 g	1 lb	1 lb
Green or red pepper, chopped (or combination of both)	1	1	1
Worcestershire sauce	3 tbsp	3 tbsp	3 tbsp
Salt and pepper			

method

1. Heat the oil in a pan and sauté the onion gently until opaque.

2. Add the rice, toss well and fry until starting to turn transparent. Pour in 600ml/1 pt/2½ cups of the stock, bring to the boil, then simmer for about 15 minutes or until most of the liquid has been absorbed.

3. Stir in the remaining ingredients and stock, cover and cook for a further 10-15 minutes, stirring occasionally until the liquid is absorbed.

4. Serve as a main meal or with chicken or curry.

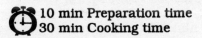 10 min Preparation time
30 min Cooking time

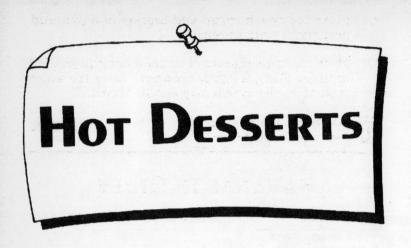

HOT DESSERTS

ALMONDINE PEACHES

ingredients	Metric	Imperial	American
Can peach halves in syrup	822 g	1 lb 13oz	1 lb 13oz
Ground almonds	25 g	1 oz	¼ cup
Caster (superfine) sugar	25 g	1 oz	2 tbsp
Butter, softened	25 g	1 oz	2 tbsp
Few drops almond essence (extract)			
Brandy or kirsch	2 tbsp	2 tbsp	2 tbsp

method

1. Drain the peaches and reserve the syrup.

2. Cream together the almonds, sugar, butter and essence.

3. Place the peach halves, rounded side down, in a flameproof dish. Spoon the almond mixture into the hollows.

4. Place the peach syrup and brandy in a pan and heat gently until warmed.

5. Flash the stuffed peaches under a hot grill (broiler) until the filling is lightly browned. Serve the sauce separately. Ice cream may also be served.

 10-15 min Preparation time
5-8 min Cooking time

BANANAS IN CIDER

ingredients	Metric	Imperial	American
Bananas	8	8	8
Grated rind and juice of 2 lemons			
Dry cider	300 ml	½ pt	1¼ cups
Brown sugar	8 tbsp	8 tbsp	8 tbsp
Ground mixed spice	1 tsp	1 tsp	1 tsp

method

1. Peel the bananas, halve and toss in lemon juice.

2. Place the lemon rind, cider, sugar and spice in a pan and heat until simmering.

3. Add the bananas to heat through. Serve with ice cream or cream.

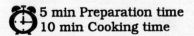 5 min Preparation time
10 min Cooking time

BRANDIED MINCEMEAT APPLES

ingredients	Metric	Imperial	American
Medium cooking (tart) apples	4	4	4
Mincemeat	6 tbsp	6 tbsp	6 tbsp
Brandy	2 tbsp	2 tbsp	2 tbsp
Apple juice	150 ml	¼ pt	⅔ cup

method

1. Core the apples, cut a narrow slit around the centre of each one and place in a shallow dish.

2. Mix the mincemeat and brandy together and pack into the apple cavities, spooning any extra on top. Pour in the apple juice.

3. Bake uncovered in the oven at 180°C/350°F/Gas Mark 4 for 35-40 minutes until tender. Serve with custard, cream or ice cream.

10 min Preparation time
35-40 min Cooking time

BRANDIED PEACH AND ALMOND CREPES

ingredients	Metric	Imperial	American
Packet pancake batter mix	30 g	½ pt	1¼ cups
Brandy	1 tbsp	1 tbsp	1 tbsp
Filling:			
Butter	100 g	4 oz	½ cup
Icing (confectioner's) sugar	50 g	2 oz	½ cup
Ground almonds	50 g	2 oz	½ cup
Few drops almond essence (extract)			
Can peach slices, drained and diced	425 g	15 oz	15 oz
Butter, melted	25 g	1 oz	2 tbsp

method

1. Make up the pancake batter mix according to directions, then stir in the brandy. Make 8 pancakes. Keep warm.

2. Cream the butter and icing sugar. Stir in the almonds, essence and peaches.

3. Divide the mixture between the pancakes and fold to form triangles.

4. Place in a flameproof dish and brush with the butter. Flash under a hot grill (broiler) and serve immediately. Accompany with fresh cream.

variation

Use canned pears or pineapple instead of peaches.

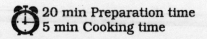
20 min Preparation time
5 min Cooking time

CHOC 'N' BANANA CREPES

ingredients	Metric	Imperial	American
Packet ready cooked crêpes	1	1	1
Plain (semi-sweet) chocolate, broken into pieces	100 g	4 oz	⅔ cup
Icing (confectioner's) sugar	50 g	2 oz	½ cup
Butter	25 g	1 oz	2 tbsp
Bananas, sliced	4	4	4
Banana yoghurt	150 g	5 oz	⅔ cup
Double (heavy) cream, whipped	150 ml	¼ pt	⅔ cup
Decoration:			
Chopped nuts	25 g	1 oz	¼ cup

method

1. Warm the crêpes according to directions.

2. Place the chocolate, icing sugar and butter in a saucepan. Heat until melted, stirring continuously.

3. Place the bananas, yoghurt and cream in a bowl and fold in to mix.

4. Layer the crêpes on a plate with the banana filling. Pour over the sauce and sprinkle with nuts. Serve immediately.

10-15 min Preparation time
5-8 min Cooking time

HOT SWISS TRIFLE

ingredients	Metric	Imperial	American
Swiss (jelly) roll	1	1	1
Can apricot halves, drained	350 g	12 oz	12 oz
425g/15 oz cans custard	2	2	2
Dried egg white	4 tsp	4 tsp	4 tsp

method

1. Slice the Swiss roll and arrange on the base and sides of a 1 litre/2 pt/ 5 cup ovenproof dish. Lay the apricots on top.

2. Heat the custard, pour over the apricots and smooth the surface.

3. Make meringue using the egg white according to directions, then pipe or swirl over the custard.

4. Cook in the oven at 180°C/350°F/Gas Mark 4 for about 10-15 minutes. The meringue may also be flashed under a hot grill (broiler) to brown the surface. Serve immediately.

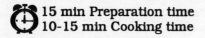 15 min Preparation time
10-15 min Cooking time

DRIED FRUIT COMPOTE

ingredients	Metric	Imperial	American
Dried fruit, such as apples, pears, prunes, bananas etc.	350 g	12 oz	2 cups
Unsweetened apple juice	600 ml	1 pt	2½ cups

method

1. Place the fruit in a bowl. Pour over the apple juice and cover. Leave to soak overnight in the refrigerator.

2. When required, pour into a pan and simmer for 20 minutes until tender.

3. Serve with fresh cream or ice cream. If wished, cool and serve chilled.

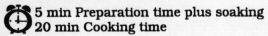 5 min Preparation time plus soaking
20 min Cooking time

JUBILEE CHERRIES

ingredients	Metric	Imperial	American
425g/15 oz cans black cherries	2	2	2
Arrowroot	2 tsp	2 tsp	2 tsp
Caster (superfine) sugar	25 g	1 oz	2 tbsp
Grated rind and juice of 1 orange			
Brandy or cherry brandy	3 tbsp	3 tbsp	3 tbsp

method

1. Drain the cherries and reserve the juice. Stone

(pit) and place the cherries in a dish.

2. Mix the arrowroot with a little cherry juice. Heat the remaining juice in a pan with the sugar, orange rind and juice.

3. Thicken with the arrowroot, add the cherries and brandy and heat through until warmed. Serve with vanilla ice cream.

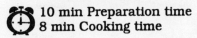 10 min Preparation time
8 min Cooking time

RHUBARB AND APPLE COBBLER

ingredients	Metric	Imperial	American
Can rhubarb	450 g	1 lb	1 lb
Can apple slices	450 g	1 lb	1 lb
Packet scone (biscuit) mix	225 g	8 oz	8 oz

method

1. Mix the rhubarb and apple together and place in an ovenproof dish.

2. Make up the scone mix according to directions and cut out 4cm/1½ inch rounds. Place the scones overlapping around the edge of the fruit, then brush with milk.

3. Bake in the oven at 200°C/400°F/Gas Mark 6 for 20 minutes until the filling is hot and the scones golden. Serve with custard, vanilla sauce or cream.

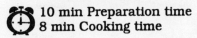 10-12 min Preparation time
20 min Cooking time

SUMMER FRUIT BRULEE

ingredients	Metric	Imperial	American
Red summer fruits, such as strawberries, raspberries, blackcurrants, etc.	450 g	1 lb	1 lb
Double (heavy) cream	150 ml	1/4 pt	2/3 cup
Natural yoghurt	150 g	5 oz	2/3 cup
Demerara sugar	50 g	2 oz	1/3 cup

method

1. Place the fruit in the base of a flameproof dish, reserving a little for decoration.

2. Whip the cream to a soft peak consistency, fold in the yoghurt and spread over the fruit.

3. Sprinkle with the sugar and place under a hot grill (broiler) until the sugar has melted and caramelized. Decorate with the reserved fruit and serve.

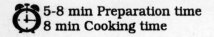 5-8 min Preparation time
8 min Cooking time

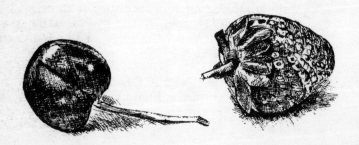

TUTTI FRUITI PASTA

ingredients	Metric	Imperial	American
Milk	900 ml	1 ½ pts	3 ¾ cups
Quick cooking pasta bows or shells	175 g	6 oz	6 oz
Sultanas (golden raisins) or raisins	50 g	2 oz	⅓ cup
Coloured or red glacé (candied) cherries, quartered	50 g	2 oz	¼ cup
Soft dark brown sugar	25 g	1 oz	2 tbsp
Flaked almonds	50 g	2 oz	½ cup
Large pinch of grated nutmeg			

method

1. Bring the milk to the boil in a pan. Add the pasta, sultanas, cherries and sugar. Simmer for 8-10 minutes, stirring frequently.

2. Add the nuts and nutmeg, then serve.

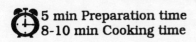
5 min Preparation time
8-10 min Cooking time

Cold
Desserts

APRICOT RICE RING

ingredients	Metric	Imperial	American
Sachet powdered gelatine	15 g	½ oz	½ oz
425g/15oz cans creamed rice	2	2	2
Vanilla essence (extract)	1 tsp	1 tsp	1 tsp
Can apricots, drained	425 g	15 oz	15 oz
Double (heavy) or whipping cream, whipped	150 ml	¼ pt	⅔ cup
Decoration:			
Cherries			
Angelica			

method

1. Dissolve the gelatine in 4 tablespoons hot water.

2. Place the creamed rice in bowl, add the vanilla essence and gelatine, then mix well.

3. Pour into a wetted 600ml/1 pt/2½ cup ring mould and chill until set.

4. Turn out, fill the centre with the apricots and decorate with cream, cherries and angelica.

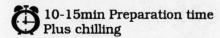 10-15min Preparation time
Plus chilling

CHESTNUT CREAM MOUSSE

ingredients	Metric	Imperial	American
Double (heavy) cream	150 ml	¼ pt	⅔ cup
Milk	1 tbsp	1 tbsp	1 tbsp
Can sweetened chestnut purée	250 g	9 oz	9 oz
Brandy or rum	3 tbsp	3 tbsp	3 tbsp
Decoration:			
Grated chocolate or flake bar			

method

1. Whisk the cream and milk together until the mixture stands in soft peaks.

2. Fold in the chestnut purée and brandy.

3. Spoon into sundae dishes and decorate with chocolate. Chill before serving.

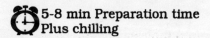 5-8 min Preparation time
Plus chilling

CHOCOLATE CREAM CUPS

ingredients	Metric	Imperial	American
Packet instant dessert mix (any flavour)	1	1	1
Box chocolate cups or shells	1	1	1
Decoration:			
Glacé (candied) cherries, angelica or grated chocolate			

method

1. Make up the instant dessert mix according to directions.

2. Pipe or spoon into the chocolate cups and decorate with cherries, angelica or grated chocolate. Chill before serving.

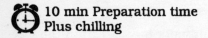 10 min Preparation time
Plus chilling

Choc 'n' Lime Mallow Flan

ingredients	Metric	Imperial	American
Butter	25 g	1 oz	2 tbsp
Plain (semisweet) chocolate	100 g	4 oz	4 oz
Digestive biscuits (Graham crackers), crumbled	225 g	8 oz	3 cups
Lemon and white marshmallows	350 g	12 oz	12 oz
Milk	150 ml	¼ pt	⅔ cup
Limes	2	2	2
Double (heavy) cream, whipped	150 ml	¼ pt	⅔ cup

method

1. Melt the butter and chocolate together, then stir in the biscuit crumbs until combined.

2. Place in a 23cm/9 inch dish and press down well to line the base and sides.

3. Wet a pair of scissors and cut the marshmallows in half. Place in a saucepan with the milk and heat gently until melted. Cool.

4. Add the grated rind and juice of 1 lime and half of the cream. Fold in until well mixed and pour over the biscuit base. Chill until set.

5. To serve, decorate with slices of lime and pipe swirls of the remaining cream.

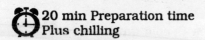 20 min Preparation time
Plus chilling

COFFEE LIQUEUR CREAM

ingredients	Metric	Imperial	American
425g/15 oz cans custard	2	2	2
Liquid coffee	3 tbsp	3 tbsp	3 tbsp
Tia Maria liqueur	2 tbsp	2 tbsp	2 tbsp
Decoration:			
Whipped cream			
Chopped nuts			

method

1. Place the custard, coffee and liqueur in a blender or food processor and mix well.

2. Pour into 4 glasses and chill.

3. Decorate with whipped cream and sprinkle with nuts. Serve with brandy snaps, langues-de-chat or ratafia biscuits.

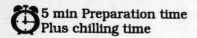 5 min Preparation time
Plus chilling time

FRUIT AND RICE RING

ingredients	Metric	Imperial	American
Can fruit pie filling	425 g	15 oz	15 oz
Can creamed rice	425 g	15 oz	15 oz
Powdered gelatine	15 g	½ oz	½ oz

method

1. Rinse a ring mould with cold water.

2. Pick the whole fruit from the syrup and place in

the bottom of the mould.

3. Mix the rice with the remainder of the fruit pie filling.

4. Dissolve the gelatine in a little hot water and stir into the rice mixture.

5. Pour into the ring mould and chill until set. Turn out on to a plate and serve.

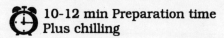 10-12 min Preparation time
Plus chilling

GOOSEBERRY FOOL

ingredients	Metric	Imperial	American
Can gooseberries	450 g	15 oz	15 oz
Can custard	450 g	15 oz	15 oz
Decoration:			
Chopped nuts	1 tbsp	1 tbsp	1 tbsp

method

1. Place the gooseberries and custard in a blender or food processor and mix until smooth.

2. Pour into sundae dishes or glasses and chill. Decorate with chopped nuts. Serve with shortbread biscuits (cookies).

variation

Use canned peaches, apricots or blackcurrants in place of gooseberries.

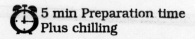 5 min Preparation time
Plus chilling

JAMAICAN MANDARIN GATEAU

ingredients	Metric	Imperial	American
Jamaican ginger cake	1	1	1
Can mandarin oranges	325 g	11 oz	11 oz
Double (heavy) cream or whipping cream	150 ml	¼ pt	⅔ cup
Grated rind of 1 orange			

method

1. Slice the cake in half lengthways and place the bottom half on a serving plate.

2. Drain the oranges and moisten each piece of cake with a little juice. Reserve a third of the oranges for decoration and chop the remainder.

3. Whip the cream until stiff with 1 tablespoon mandarin juice and the grated orange rind. Place half in a piping (pastry) bag. Fold the chopped oranges into the remaining cream and spread over the base of the cake. Position on the cake top.

4. Decorate each top edge of the gâteau with piped cream and arrange the reserved oranges in the centre. Chill before serving.

variation

Use canned peaches, pineapple or pears and omit the orange rind.

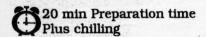 20 min Preparation time
Plus chilling

JAMAICAN PEAR TRIFLE

ingredients	Metric	Imperial	American
Can pear halves in syrup	800 g	1¾ lb	1¾ lb
Jamaican ginger cake	1	1	1
Rum	2-3 tbsp	2-3 tbsp	2-3 tbsp
Carton custard	1 litre	1 ¾ pts	4 ¼ cups
Double (heavy) cream, whipped	150 ml	¼ pt	⅔ cup
Chopped nuts	25 g	1 oz	¼ cup

method

1. Drain the pears and reserve the syrup.

2. Slice the ginger cake and arrange the slices on the base and sides of a glass serving dish.

3. Mix the pear syrup and rum and pour over the cake. Arrange the pears on top.

4. Pour the custard over the pears and level with a palette knife (metal spatula).

5. Spread or pipe the cream in swirls over the custard. Sprinkle with chopped nuts. Serve chilled.

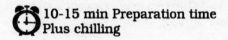 10-15 min Preparation time
Plus chilling

LEMONY CUSTARD SLICE

ingredients	Metric	Imperial	American
Caster (superfine) sugar	50 g	2 oz	¼ cup
Eggs, size 3	2	2	2
Flour	50 g	2 oz	½ cup
Milk	300 ml	½ pt	1¼ cups
Single (light) cream	225 ml	8 fl oz	1 cup
Grated rind of ½ lemon			
Ground cinnamon	½ tsp	½ tsp	½ tsp
To serve:			
Can blackberries, blackcurrants or black cherries	425 g	15 oz	15 oz

method

1. Beat the sugar and eggs together in a bowl until pale and fluffy. Whisk in the flour, milk, cream, lemon rind and cinnamon.

2. Pour the mixture into a buttered shallow square ovenproof dish. Bake in the oven at 180°C/ 350°F/Gas Mark 4 for 50-60 minutes until set and golden brown. Chill when cool.

3. Cut the slice into squares and serve with canned fruit or pie filling.

variation

Jars or cans of pie filling may also be used to serve.

🕐 10-15 min Preparation time
50-60min Cooking time
Plus chilling

MARSHMALLOW ICE CREAM

ingredients	Metric	Imperial	American
Pink and white marshmallows	100 g	4 oz	4 oz
Milk	150 ml	¼ pt	⅔ cup
Eggs, size 3	2	2	2
Icing (confectioner's) sugar	25 g	1 oz	¼ cup
Pistachio essence (extract)	1 tsp	1 tsp	1 tsp
Double (heavy) cream, whipped	150 ml	¼ pt	⅔ cup

method

1. Wet a pair of scissors and cut the marshmallows in half. Place in a saucepan with the milk and heat gently until melted. Cool.

2. Place the eggs, icing sugar and essence in a bowl and whisk until thick and creamy.

3. Fold in the whipped cream and marshmallow mixture. Pour into a freezer tray and freezer until set 1cm/½ inch around the edges.

4. Spoon into a bowl, break up the mixture and stir until smooth.

5. Return to a clean freezer tray and freeze until firm - about 2 hours. Serve with fantail biscuits (cookies).

variation

Substitute pistachio essence with maraschino essence.

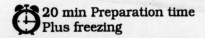 20 min Preparation time
Plus freezing

ORANGES CASSATA

ingredients	Metric	Imperial	American
Large oranges	4	4	4
Double (heavy) or whipping cream	300 ml	½ pt	1 ¼ cups
Chopped nuts	50 g	2 oz	½ cup
Coloured glacé (candied) cherries, chopped	50 g	2 oz	¼ cup
Plain (semisweet) chocolate, coarsely grated or finely chopped	50 g	2 oz	⅓ cup
Sultanas (golden raisins)	50 g	2 oz	⅓ cup
Few drops orange liqueur or rum			

method

1. Slice the top off each orange and, using a sharp knife, cut the flesh from the inside and chop.

2. Reserve 2 tablespoons orange juice and replace the remainder and flesh in the base of each orange shell.

3. Whip the cream with the orange juice until stiff. Fold in nuts, cherries, chocolate, sultanas and liqueur or rum if used.

4. Spoon the cream mixture into the oranges and chill.

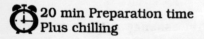
20 min Preparation time
Plus chilling

ORANGE MOUSSE

ingredients	Metric	Imperial	American
Packet orange jelly (orange flavor gelatin)	½	½	½
Milk	300 ml	½ pt	1¼ cups
Orange yoghurt	150 g	5 oz	⅔ cup
Natural yoghurt	150 g	5 oz	⅔ cup
Decoration:			
Angelica leaves			
Glacé (candied) cherries			

method

1. Break the jelly into cubes and place in a heatproof bowl with 4 tablespoons water.

2. Dissolve by stirring over a pan of boiling water. Leave to cool, but not to set.

3. Whisk the cooled jelly with the milk and yoghurt until frothy. Pour into glasses or sundae dishes and chill to set.

4. Decorate with glacé cherries and angelica leaves.

variation

Substitute the orange jelly and yoghurt for strawberry, peach or lemon flavour.

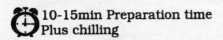
10-15min Preparation time
Plus chilling

PEAR AND WALNUT COMPOTE

ingredients	Metric	Imperial	American
Can pear halves	550 g	1¼ lb	1¼ lb
Red wine	300 ml	½ pt	1¼ cups
Ground cinnamon	1 tsp	1 tsp	1 tsp
Grated nutmeg	1 tsp	1 tsp	1 tsp
Walnuts, chopped	50 g	2 oz	½ cup

method

1. Drain the pears and reserve 150ml/¼ pint/⅔ cup of the juice.

2. Place the pears, reserved juice, wine, cinnamon and nutmeg in a pan. Bring to the boil, cover and simmer gently for 10 minutes.

3. Add the walnuts and leave to cool. Serve chilled with cream.

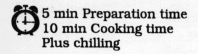 5 min Preparation time
10 min Cooking time
Plus chilling

PINEAPPLE CRUNCH LAYER

ingredients	Metric	Imperial	American
Digestive biscuits (Graham crackers), crushed	150 g	5 oz	2 cups
Butter, melted	50 g	2 oz	¼ cup
Can pineapple pieces, drained	350 g	12 oz	12 oz
Can custard	425 g	15 oz	15 oz
Decoration:			
Aerosol can cream			

method

1. Mix the biscuit crumbs and butter and place half in the bottom of 4 sundae glasses.

2. Fold the pineapple into the custard, reserving a few pieces for decoration, then spread over the biscuit base.

3. Top with the remaining biscuit crumb. Pipe a swirl of cream and decorate with the remaining pineapple. Chill before serving.

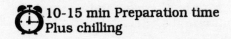 10-15 min Preparation time
Plus chilling

RHUBARB GINGER LAYER CREAM

ingredients	Metric	Imperial	American
Ginger biscuits (cookies), crushed	*100 g*	*4 oz*	*1½ cups*
Double (heavy) or whipping cream	*150 ml*	*¼ pt*	*⅔ cup*
Raspberry or rhubarb yoghurt	*150 g*	*5 oz*	*⅔ cup*
Can rhubarb, puréed	*425 g*	*15 oz*	*15 oz*

method

1. Place the biscuits in a plastic bag and crush using a rolling pin. Reserve 2 teaspoons for decoration.

2. Whip the cream until thick and place 2 tablespoons in a piping (pastry) bag for decoration. Mix the remainder with the yoghurt and rhubarb.

3. Arrange layers of biscuit crumbs and rhubarb cream between 4 glasses or sundae dishes. Decorate with a rosette of cream and a sprinkling of reserved biscuit crumbs. Serve chilled.

variation

Use digestive biscuits (Graham crackers) instead of ginger ones.

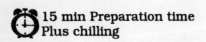 15 min Preparation time
Plus chilling

RICE CASSATA MOULD

ingredients	Metric	Imperial	American
Can creamed rice	425 g	15 oz	15 oz
Natural yoghurt	150 g	5 oz	⅔ cup
Coloured glacé (candied) cherries, chopped	50 g	2 oz	¼ cup
Chopped nuts	50 g	2 oz	½ cup
Sultanas (golden raisins)	50 g	2 oz	⅓ cup
Powdered gelatine	15 g	½ oz	½ oz
Decoration:			
Bought ice cream sauce			
Whipped cream			
Glacé (candied) cherries			

method

1. Mix the rice pudding, yoghurt, cherries, nuts and sultanas together.

2. Dissolve the gelatine in a little hot water and add to the rice mixture, stirring well.

3. Pour into a 600ml/1 pint/2 ½ cup wetted jelly mould or 4 dariole moulds and chill until set.

4. Turn out and decorate the top with ice cream sauce, whipped cream and glacé cherries.

10-15 min Preparation time
Plus chilling

SNOWCAP PEAK

ingredients	Metric	Imperial	American
White wine	90 ml	3 fl oz	6 tbsp
Grated rind and juice of 1 lemon			
Caster (superfine) sugar	75 g	3 oz	6 tbsp
Double (heavy) cream	300 ml	½ pt	1¼ cups
Decoration:			
Cocktail cherries	4	4	4
Angelica leaves			

method

1. Place the wine, lemon rind and juice and sugar in a bowl. Leave to stand for at least 2 hours.

2. Add the cream and whisk until the mixture thickens and stands in peaks.

3. Divide between 4 sundae dishes or glasses. Decorate with cherries and angelica leaves. Chill before serving. Serve with crisp biscuits (cookies), such as shortbread fingers or langues de chats.

variation

Use cider instead of white wine.

5-8 min Preparation time
Plus standing and chilling

SWISS ROLL BOMBE

ingredients	Metric	Imperial	American
Swiss (jelly) rolls	2	2	2
Thick custard, cooled	300 ml	½ pt	1¼ cups
Whipping cream, whipped	150 ml	¼ pt	⅔ cup
Strawberry yoghurt	150 g	5 oz	⅔ cup
Strawberries, fresh, frozen or canned	450 g	1 lb	1 lb

method

1. Slice both Swiss rolls into 1cm/½ inch slices and use to line a 600ml/1 pint/2 ½ cup basin.

2. Mix the custard, cream and yoghurt together and pour into the basin.

3. Place in the refrigerator and leave to set - about 2 hours.

4. Turn out on to a plate and serve sliced in wedges with the strawberries.

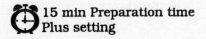 15 min Preparation time
Plus setting

WALNUT CHEESE BOMBE

ingredients	Metric	Imperial	American
White Stilton cheese	225 g	8 oz	8 oz
Caerphilly cheese	225 g	8 oz	8 oz
Red or white port	4 tbsp	4 tbsp	4 tbsp
Walnuts, finely chopped	100 g	4 oz	1 cup
Garnish:			
Parsley sprigs			

method

1. Crumble the cheeses into a blender or food processor, add the port and mix until smooth.

2. Place the cheese mixture into a bowl and stir in half of the walnuts.

3. Turn onto waxed paper or clingfilm (plastic wrap) and shape into a ball. Coat in the remaining walnuts and chill before serving.

4. Garnish with parsley and serve on its own with biscuits or with a cheese board.

variation

Serve the bombe as a starter.

15 min Preparation time
Plus chilling

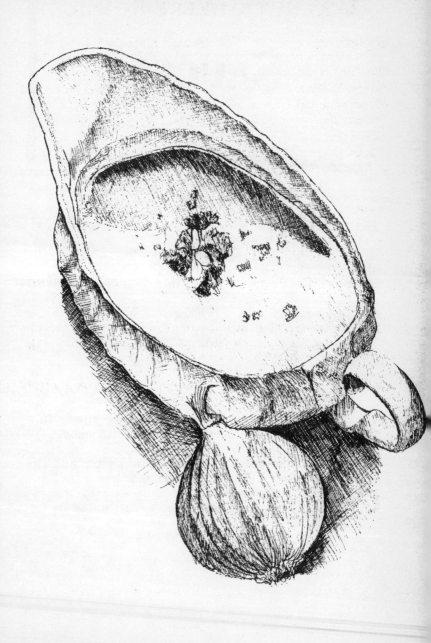

SAUCES

BLACKCURRANT AND ORANGE SAUCE

ingredients	Metric	Imperial	American
Can blackcurrants *Grated rind and juice of* *1 orange*	450 g	1 lb	1 lb

method

1. Place the blackcurrants, including juice, in a blender or food processor and mix until smooth.

2. Strain to remove the blackcurrant pips. add the orange rind and juice and mix well

3. Serve hot or cold with fresh fruit salad or ice cream.

 8 min Preparation time

Chocolate Orange Sauce

ingredients	Metric	Imperial	American
Plain (semisweet) or milk chocolate, broken into pieces	50 g	2 oz	1/3 cup
Butter	15 g	1/2 oz	1 tbsp
Golden (light corn) syrup	4 tbsp	4 tbsp	4 tbsp
Grated rind of 1 orange			

method

1. Place all the ingredients in a heatproof bowl over a pan of hot water.

2. Leave to melt, then beat until smooth.

3. Serve with ice cream, cold desserts or profiteroles.

variation

Substitute orange rind with lemon or lime rind.

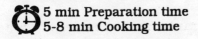 5 min Preparation time
5-8 min Cooking time

171

COLD MUSTARD SAUCE

ingredients	Metric	Imperial	American
Soured cream	150 ml	¼ pt	⅔ cup
Medium onion, finely chopped	1	1	1
Mustard, such as wholegrain, German, English	1 tbsp	1 tbsp	1 tbsp
Salt and pepper			

method

1. Place all the ingredients in a bowl and mix well. Chill.

2. Serve with cold meats and sausages or with jacket or new potatoes.

5 min Preparation time
Plus chilling

HOT AND SPICY BARBECUE SAUCE

ingredients	Metric	Imperial	American
Butter	25 g	1 oz	2 tbsp
Small onion, finely chopped	1	1	1
Worcestershire sauce	1 tbsp	1 tbsp	1 tbsp
Tomato ketchup	2 tbsp	2 tbsp	2 tbsp
Lemon juice	1 tbsp	1 tbsp	1 tbsp
Demerara sugar	1 tbsp	1 tbsp	1 tbsp
Clove garlic, crushed (optional)	1	1	1
Natural yoghurt	150 g	5 oz	⅔ cup
Salt and pepper			

method

1. Melt the butter in a pan and sauté the onion until tender and turning brown.

2. Remove from the heat and stir in the Worcestershire sauce, ketchup, lemon juice, sugar, garlic, yoghurt and seasoning.

3. Heat gently until the ingredients are blended and the sugar has dissolved. Do not allow to boil.

4. This sauce is ideal for basting sausages and hamburgers during grilling or barbecuing. Serve any remaining sauce separately.

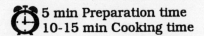
5 min Preparation time
10-15 min Cooking time

LEMON AND GINGER MARINADE

ingredients	Metric	Imperial	American
Oil	4 tbsp	4 tbsp	4 tbsp
Brown sugar	1 tbsp	1 tbsp	1 tbsp
Ground ginger	2 tsp	2 tsp	2 tsp
Grated rind and juice of 1 lemon			

method

1. Place all the ingredients in a bowl and mix well.

2. Use to marinate lamb chops, beef steaks or kebabs for 2-3 hours before cooking. Baste with the marinade during cooking.

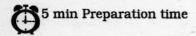 5 min Preparation time

MAYONNAISE IDEAS

Flavour mayonnaise with any of the following ingredients to give a variation for salad dressings:

> Curry powder or paste
> Mustard (prepared)
> Cayenne or paprika pepper
> Garlic purée
> Tomato purée (paste)
> Lemon juice
> Fresh or dried herbs
> Chopped gherkins (dill pickles) or capers
> Sour cream may also be used in place of mayonnaise.

MOCHA SAUCE

ingredients	Metric	Imperial	American
Demerara sugar	50 g	2 oz	1/3 cup
Strong black coffee	2 tsp	2 tsp	2 tsp
Butter	15 g	1/2 oz	1 tbsp
Plain (semisweet) chocolate, broken	100 g	4 oz	2/3 cup

method

1. Place all the ingredients in a pan and heat gently until the sauce is smooth, stirring continuously.

2. Serve with profiteroles, ice cream or meringues.

⏰ 3-5 min Preparation time
5 min Cooking time

MUSTARD AND TOMATO RELISH

ingredients	Metric	Imperial	American
Tomato juice	150 ml	¼ pt	⅔ cup
Small onion, finely chopped	1	1	1
Wholegrain mustard	1 tsp	1 tsp	1 tsp
Mixed herbs	½ tsp	½ tsp	½ tsp
Salt and pepper			

method

1. Place all the ingredients in a bowl and mix well.

2. Serve with kebabs, burgers or sausages.

 5 min Preparation time

PERKY PLUM SAUCE

ingredients	Metric	Imperial	American
Can red plum halves, stones (pits) removed	550 g	1¼ lb	1¼ lb
Wholegrain mustard	1 tbsp	1 tbsp	1 tbsp
Sherry or port	2 tbsp	2 tbsp	2 tbsp
Cornflour (cornstarch)	2 tbsp	2 tbsp	2 tbsp

method

1. Place the plums, juice, mustard and sherry in a blender or food processor and mix until smooth.

2. Pour into a saucepan and bring to the boil. Mix the cornflour with a little water and use to thicken the sauce.

3. Serve with cold ham, turkey, chicken or pork. The sauce may also be served cold.

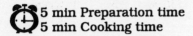 5 min Preparation time
5 min Cooking time

SPEEDY BARBECUE SAUCE

ingredients	Metric	Imperial	American
Butter	50 g	2 oz	¼ cup
Large onion, finely chopped	1	1	1
Can chopped tomatoes	425 g	15 oz	15 oz
Worcestershire sauce	2 tbsp	2 tbsp	2 tbsp
Honey	1 tbsp	1 tbsp	1 tbsp
Salt and pepper			
Clove garlic, crushed (optional) or pinch of garlic powder	1	1	1

method

1. Place all the ingredients in a pan. Bring to the boil, cover and simmer for 20 minutes.

2. Use for basting chicken while grilling (broiling) or barbecuing. Serve any remaining sauce separately.

5 min Preparation time
20 min Cooking time

WHITE SAUCE - SAVOURY

Flavour a packet of white sauce mix with any of the
following ingredients to give a variation:

Fresh or dried herbs
Grated cheese
Horseradish sauce
Mustard (prepared)
Onion flakes
Breadcrumbs or stuffing mix
Lemon rind and juice
Chopped gherkins (dill pickles) or capers

WHITE SAUCE - SWEET

Flavour a packet of white sauce mix with any of the
following ingredients to give a variation:

Essences (extracts) and colourings
Grated orange rind
Grated lemon rind
Liqueurs or spirits
Chopped maraschino cherries
Chopped ginger in syrup
Chopped mixed peel

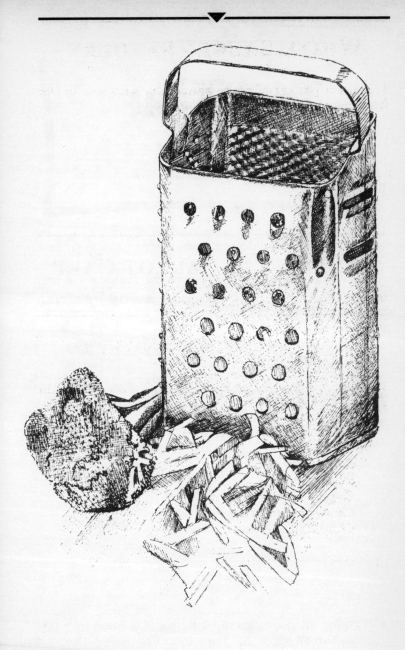

TEA-TIME BAKES

BANANA AND CARROT CAKE

ingredients	Metric	Imperial	American
Wholemeal flour	225 g	8 oz	2 cups
Light brown sugar	100 g	4 oz	⅔ cup
Bananas, mashed	2	2	2
Carrots, grated	175 g	6 oz	1½ cups
Sunflower oil	175 ml	6 floz	¾ cup
Raisins	50 g	2 oz	⅓ cup
Ground mixed spice	1 tsp	1 tsp	1 tsp
Baking powder	2 tsp	2 tsp	2 tsp
Icing:			
Icing (confectioner's) sugar, sifted	125 g	4 oz	1 cup
Grated rind and juice of 1 orange			

method

1. Place all the cake ingredients in a bowl and mix well until smooth. Turn into a prepared 18cm/ 7 inch cake tin (pan) and smooth the surface.

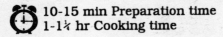

2. Bake in the oven at 180°C/350°F/Gas Mark 4 for 1-1 ¼ hours.

3. When cool, mix the icing sugar and orange rind and juice together and spread over the top of the cake.

⏰ 10-15 min Preparation time
1-1¼ hr Cooking time

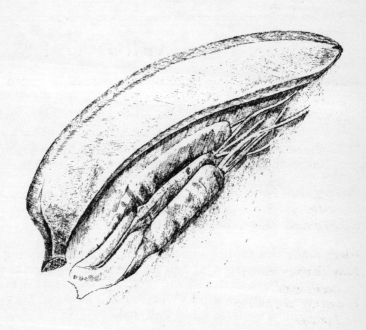

CHERRY AND ALMOND SCONES

ingredients	Metric	Imperial	American
Self-raising flour	225 g	8 oz	2 cups
Baking powder	1 tsp	1 tsp	1 tsp
Butter	50 g	2 oz	¼ cup
Glacé (candied) cherries, quartered	50 g	2 oz	¼ cup
Flaked almonds	25 g	1 oz	2 tbsp
Few drops almond essence (extract)			
Milk	150 ml	¼ pt	⅔ cup
Milk to glaze			

method

1. Place all the ingredients in a bowl, adding sufficient milk to mix to a soft dough.

2. Knead lightly and roll out to 1.25cm/½ inch thickness. Cut into 6.5cm/2 ½ inch rounds using a fluted cutter. Re-roll the trimmings.

3. Place the scones (biscuits) on a greased baking tray and brush with milk. Bake in the oven on the shelf above centre at 220°C/425°F/Gas Mark 7 for 10-12 minutes until well risen and golden. Serve warm or cool, split and buttered.

Makes 12

10-15 min Preparation time
10-12 min Cooking time

CHOCOLATE CUP CAKES

ingredients	Metric	Imperial	American
Butter	100 g	4 oz	½ cup
Caster (superfine) sugar	100 g	4 oz	½ cup
Plain (all-purpose) flour, sieved	150 g	5 oz	1¼ cups
Cocoa powder, sieved	25 g	1 oz	¼ cup
Baking powder	1 tsp	1 tsp	1 tsp
Eggs, size 3	2	2	2
Milk	1 tbsp	1 tbsp	1 tbsp
Icing:			
Plain (semisweet) chocolate or white cooking chocolate	100 g	4 oz	⅔ cup
Butter	15 g	½ oz	1 tbsp
Icing (confectioner's) sugar, sieved	175 g	6 oz	1 ½ cups
Milk	1-2 tbsp	1-2 tbsp	1-2 tbsp

method

1. Place all the cake ingredients in a bowl and beat for 2 minutes until smooth.

2. Spoon the mixture into paper cake cases. Bake in the oven on the shelf above centre at 190°C/375°F/Gas Mark 5 for 15-20 minutes. Cool.

3. For the icing, place the chocolate and butter in a heatproof bowl over a pan of hot water and stir until melted.

4. Add the sugar and beat until smooth, adding enough milk to make a spreading consistency.

5. Spread over the top of each cake.

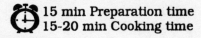

variation

Add a flavouring of choice to the icing, such as peppermint, orange, lemon, etc.

If white chocolate is used, food colouring may be added.

Makes about 16 cakes

⏰ 15 min Preparation time
15-20 min Cooking time

FRUIT 'N' NUT SLICE

ingredients	Metric	Imperial	American
Butter	100 g	4 oz	½ cup
Caster (superfine) sugar	25 g	1 oz	2 tbsp
Chocolate (plain or milk)	25 g	1 oz	1 oz
Golden (light corn) syrup	1 tbsp	1 tbsp	1 tbsp
Mixed dried fruit	50 g	2 oz	⅓ cup
Chopped nuts	25 g	1 oz	¼ cup
Glacé (candied) cherries, chopped	25 g	1 oz	1 tbsp
Digestive biscuits (Graham crackers), crushed	225 g	8 oz	3 cups
Decoration:			
Chocolate, plain (semisweet) or milk	100 g	4 oz	⅔ cup

method

1. Place the butter, sugar, chocolate and syrup in a pan and heat until melted. Add the mixed fruit, nuts and cherries.

2. Add the biscuits, stir well until combined and smooth.

3. Turn the mixture into an 18cm/7 inch square tin (pan). Level the surface and chill.

4. Melt the chocolate in a heatproof bowl over a pan of hot water. Spread over the biscuit base and chill. Serve cut into squares or fingers.

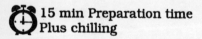 15 min Preparation time
Plus chilling

LEMON SHORTBREAD

ingredients	Metric	Imperial	American
Butter	225 g	8 oz	1 cup
Icing (confectioner's) sugar	100 g	4 oz	1 cup
Plain (all-purpose) flour	225 g	8 oz	2 cups
Cornflour (cornstarch)	100 g	4 oz	1 cup
Grated rind of 1 lemon			
Caster (superfine) sugar to sprinkle			

method

1. Cream the butter and sugar until light and fluffy.

2. Add the remaining ingredients and mix to form a dough.

3. Press the mixture into a greased Swiss roll tin (jelly roll pan) measuring 18cm x 27.5cm/7 x 11 inches. Bake in the oven at 170°C/325°F/Gas Mark 3 for 40 minutes until golden. Sprinkle with caster sugar while still warm and mark into 16 fingers.

variation

Substitute lemon rind with orange rind.

🕐 10 min Preparation time
40 min Cooking time

INDEX